For my children. I love you with all my heart.

— CP

Contents

Papacy Basics

The Pope as Monarch

Pope as Head of Church

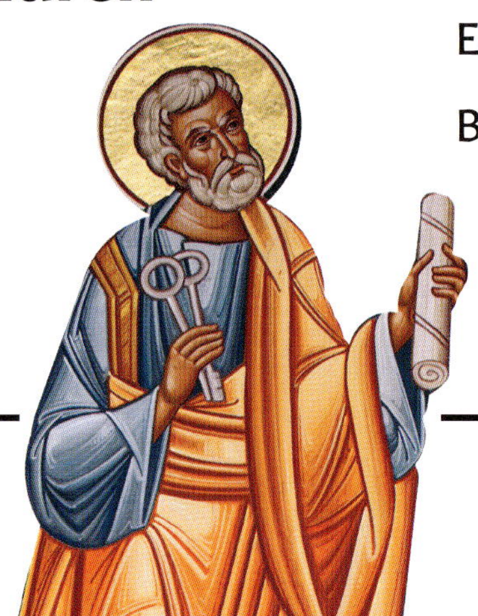

OSV kids DISCOVER

THE POPE

COLLEEN PRESSPRICH

OSV kids
Huntington, Indiana

30 29 28 27 26 25 1 2 3 4 5 6 7 8 9

Our Sunday Visitor Publishing Division
Our Sunday Visitor, Inc.
200 Noll Plaza
Huntington, IN 46750
www.osv.com
1-800-348-2440

ISBN: 978-1-63966-069-8 (Inventory No. T2810)
1. JUVENILE NONFICTION—Religion—Christianity.
2. JUVENILE NONFICTION—Religious—Christian—Learning Concepts.
3. RELIGION—Christianity—Catholic.

LCCN: 2024936407

Cover and interior design: Lindsey Riesen
Cover photos: Dieter Philippi, *Red Loafer* of Pope Benedict XVI, Creative Commons share-alike 3.0 license; *Swis Guard*-Alessia Giuliani / CPP; *Papal seal*-The Portable Antiquities Scheme/ The Trustees of the British Museum, *Popemobile*-Creative Commons Share Alike 2.0 license; *Papal Bull*-The Catholic news agency of the Bishops' Conference of Bosnia and Herzegovina; photograph by Livioandronico 2013, Creative Commons 4.0 International license; *Pope Leo's Ring*–From *Nordisk Familjebok*, vol. 8 (1908) on runeberg.org; if not noted-Adobe Stock

Printed in Turkey by PrintCenter

Papal Daily Life

Becoming Pope

A Timeline of Popes

Papacy Basics

What Is the Papacy?

"And I tell you, you are Peter, and on this rock I will build my Church, and the gates of Hades shall not prevail against it. I will give you the keys of the kingdom of heaven, and whatever you bind on earth shall be bound in heaven, and whatever you loose on earth shall be loosed in heaven." (Matthew 16:18–19)

FUN FACT

The word *pope* comes from the Latin word *papa* which is derived from the Greek word for "father."

Over the two thousand years since Jesus announced that he was going to build his Church upon Saint Peter, there have been hundreds of men who have held the title of Pope.

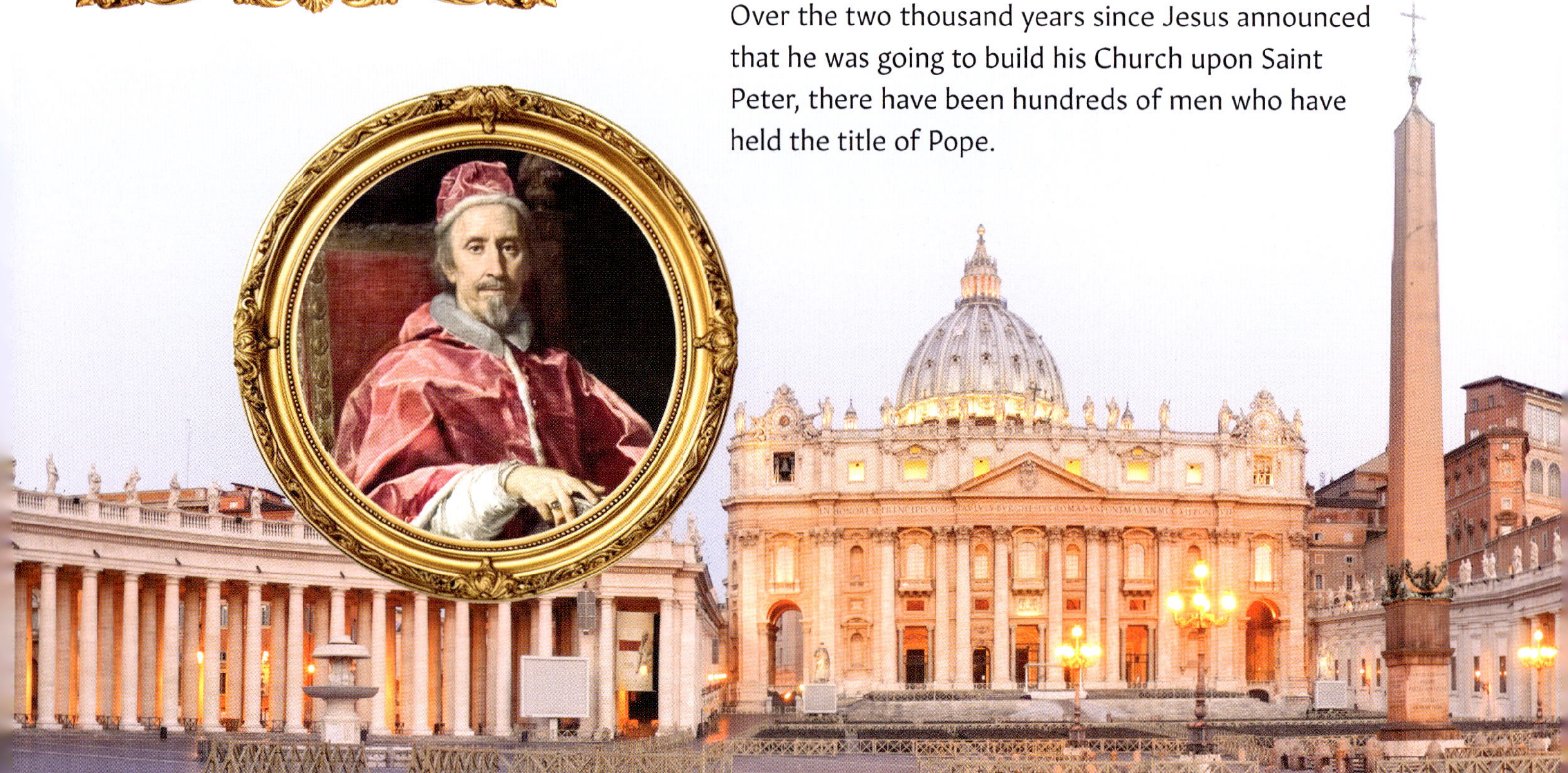

The pope is the successor to Saint Peter. He is the Bishop of Rome and the spiritual head of the Catholic Church. He has authority over Catholics and can exercise infallibility in matters of faith and morals. The pope is both a head of state (he's the ruler of Vatican City) and head of the Church.

Symbols of the Papacy

Keys to the Kingdom

Jesus told Peter that he would receive the keys to the kingdom of heaven. These keys are a symbol of the pope's authority to loose and bind sins.

The Papal Tiara

The papal tiara is a three-tiered crown that is a symbol of the pope's authority. Historically, it was worn at the coronation of the pope and other formal occasions. Pope Pius VI was the last pope to be crowned with the tiara, and none have been worn by popes since him.

Just as kings and queens have multiple tiaras and crowns available for their use, so does the pope.

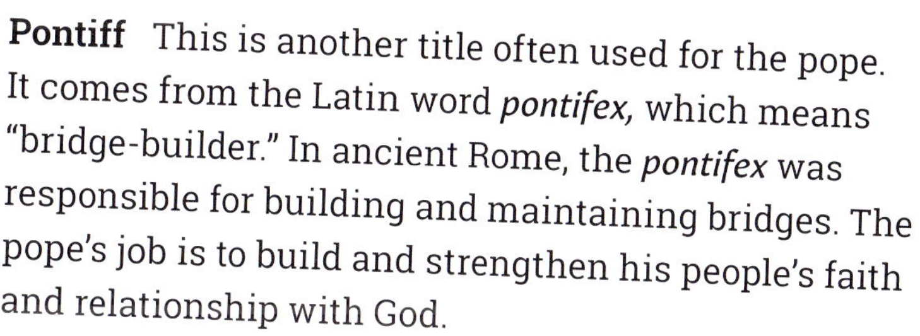

Pontiff This is another title often used for the pope. It comes from the Latin word *pontifex,* which means "bridge-builder." In ancient Rome, the *pontifex* was responsible for building and maintaining bridges. The pope's job is to build and strengthen his people's faith and relationship with God.

Who Is the Pope?

The pope is the head of the Catholic Church and the monarch of Vatican City. He is the successor to Saint Peter, the first pope and the person to whom Jesus gave the keys to the kingdom of heaven.

The Pope Is the Bishop of Rome

In addition to being the head of the entire Catholic Church, the pope is also a bishop: the Bishop of Rome. As such, he is in charge of the Diocese of Rome in a particular way as their shepherd.

FUN FACT

The pope is an elected monarch, which is rare. Usually, a monarch (a king or queen) inherits their title and position, but each pope is chosen individually.

King Charles III of the United Kingdom inherited the title of king when his mother, Queen Elizabeth II died.

Who Can Become the Pope?

Any male who has been baptized Catholic can become pope.

YES, BUT

Every pope since 1378, when Pope Urban VI was elected, has been a cardinal.

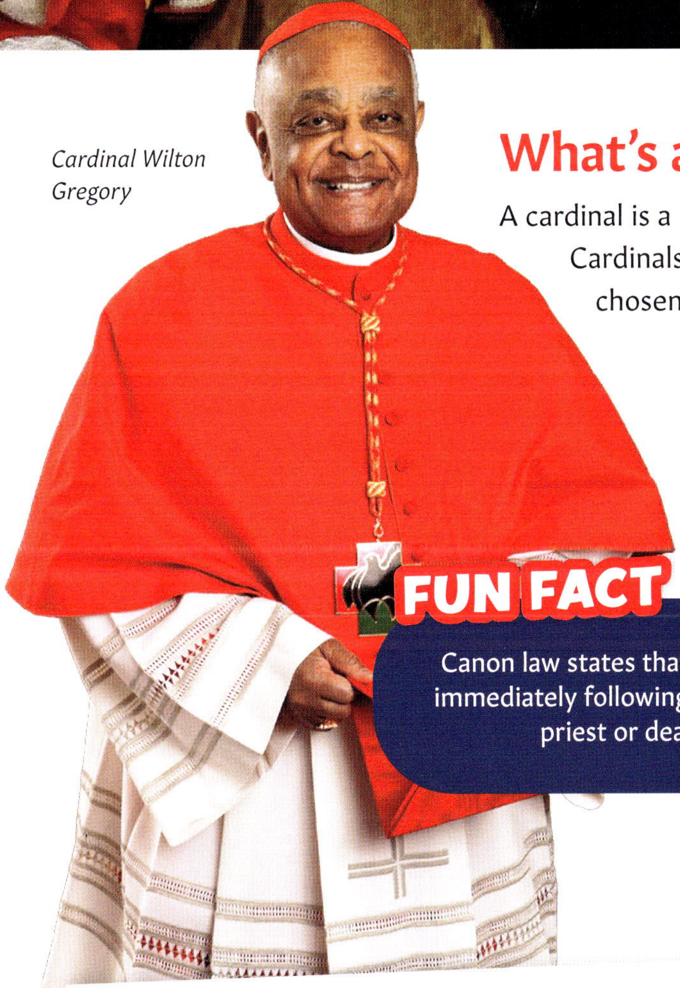

Cardinal Wilton Gregory

What's a Cardinal?

A cardinal is a rank of honor within the Catholic Church. Cardinals are priests or bishops and have been chosen by the pope. They hold the title for life.

Cardinals, like the bird of the same name, wear red.

FUN FACT

Canon law states that if a bishop or cardinal is elected pope, he becomes pope immediately following his election. But, if a man who isn't already a bishop (or a priest or deacon) is elected, he needs to be consecrated first.

Canon Law the laws governing the Catholic Church

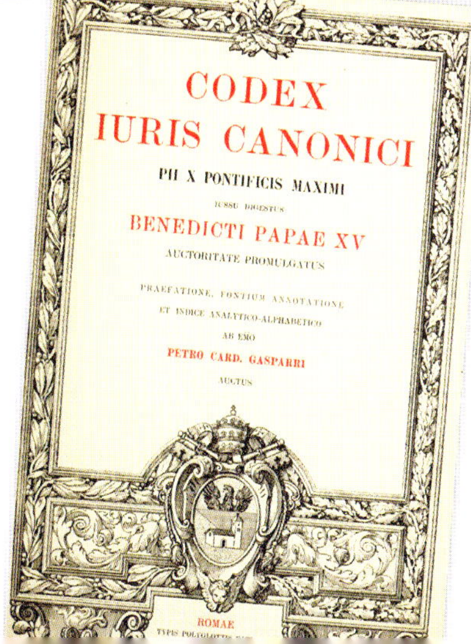

CODEX
IURIS CANONICI
PII X PONTIFICIS MAXIMI
IUSSU DIGESTUS
BENEDICTI PAPAE XV
AUCTORITATE PROMULGATUS
PRAEFATIONE, FONTIUM ANNOTATIONE
ET INDICE ANALYTICO-ALPHABETICO
AB EMO
PETRO CARD. GASPARRI
AUCTUS
ROMAE

In 1917, the first complete collection of laws of the Roman Catholic Church was compiled in Latin. It was revised in 1983.

Peter, the First Pope

Peter, originally named Simon, was one of the twelve apostles of Christ. He is known as the first pope of the Catholic Church, though he wouldn't have recognized the title.

A simple fisherman from Galilee with little to no formal education, Peter was the unlikely man chosen to lead the band of apostles and, later, the new Christians.

The Ancient Galilee Boat

This ancient fishing boat was discovered in 1986 in the Sea of Galilee. Scholars have dated it as being from the first century AD, and it would have been the type of boat used by Jesus and his apostles in the Gospels.

Who Was Peter's Wife?

The Gospels tell us that Jesus healed Peter's mother-in-law, which means the apostle must have been married. Some historians believe that Peter's wife died before he met Jesus. Some, however, say that not only did she live, she was martyred alongside him. Eusebius, a Roman historian, says: *"They say, accordingly, that when the blessed Peter saw his own wife led out to die, he rejoiced because of her summons and her return home, and called to her very encouragingly and comfortingly, addressing her by name, and saying, 'Oh thou, remember the Lord.' Such was the marriage of the blessed, and their perfect disposition toward those dearest to them."*

Peter in the Gospels

Called to follow Jesus with his brother Andrew, Peter became one of Jesus' closest companions. Along with James and John, Peter was chosen among the apostles to be with Jesus during key, private moments — for example, the Transfiguration and in the Garden of Gethsemane.

191

The number of times Peter's name is mentioned in the Gospels. This is more often than any of the other apostles.

Peter's New Name

When Jesus asks his followers, "Who do you say that I am?" it is Peter who announces, "You are the Christ," earning him a new name and Jesus' pronouncement, "On this rock, I will build my Church."

Cephas The word Cephas comes from the Aramaic word for rock. Aramaic would have been the language spoken by Jesus and his apostles.

Peter's Denial

On the night before Jesus was crucified, Peter denied being a follower of Jesus three times. This denial, predicted by Jesus at the Last Supper, Peter later bitterly regretted.

After his resurrection, Jesus offered Peter an opportunity to redeem that denial and express his love for his Savior by asking him three times if he loved him.

Leader of a New Church

The Acts of the Apostles tells the story of the early Church. In it, we can see that Peter is the leader of the band of apostles following Jesus' resurrection and ascension.

Peter ran the election of Matthias, who was chosen to replace Judas as an apostle. He was the first to preach to the crowds at Pentecost. And later, he defended the rest of the apostles in front of the Jewish court.

Pentecost is known as the birthday of the Church. Filled with the Holy Spirit, Peter left the Upper Room where the apostles had been praying, and went out to the people, preaching to them in their own languages.

Peter's Arrest

According to the Book of Acts, Peter was put into prison by King Herod, probably in about the year AD 44. The night before he was supposed to go on trial, an angel appeared to him. The chains that bound his hands miraculously fell off and he was able to follow the angel through the unlocked doors and out of the prison.

Peter's Death

Historians believe Saint Peter was martyred in Rome between AD 64 and 68 during the reign of the Emperor Nero.

Tradition tells us that St. Peter was crucified upside down, at his request, because he did not feel worthy to die in the same way that Jesus did.

Martyr someone who dies for his or her faith

Emperor Nero is most remembered today for his persecution of Christians. When a fire burned down a large portion of Rome in AD 64, Nero publicly claimed that followers of this new religion were to blame.

The Pope as Monarch

The Papal States

Also called the Republic of Saint Peter

The Papal States were a set of territories in central Italy that recognized the pope as monarch and ruler.

Formed 756
Disbanded 1870

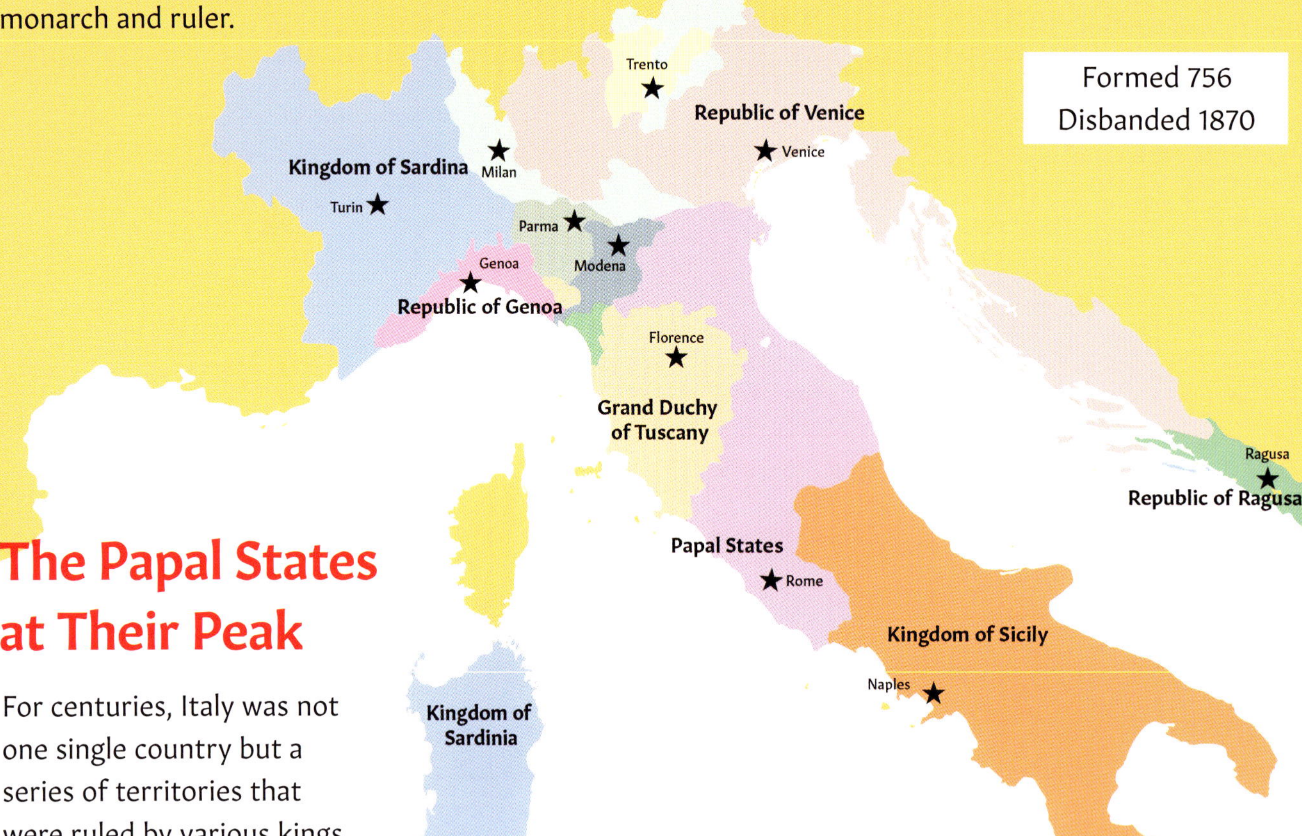

The Papal States at Their Peak

For centuries, Italy was not one single country but a series of territories that were ruled by various kings, emperors, and local leaders. The Papal States were one set of such territories.

The Beginnings

In the fifth century, as the Roman authority broke down, the people of Italy began to look to the pope for protection against invasions.

Pope Leo I successfully kept Rome out of the control of Attila the Hun. Pope Gregory I was likewise successful in keeping back the Lombards, a Germanic people who sought to conquer Italy.

For centuries after the fall of Rome in AD 476, popes were allies of the Byzantine Empire.

The Byzantine Empire at Its Peak

The Byzantine Empire, like the Roman Empire before it, included large territories of land. This map shows the Byzantine Empire at the peak of its power, including what we now know as the country of Italy. The capital of the Byzantine Empire was Constantinople.

But in the eighth century, the emperor in Constantinople clashed with the pope on three important subjects:

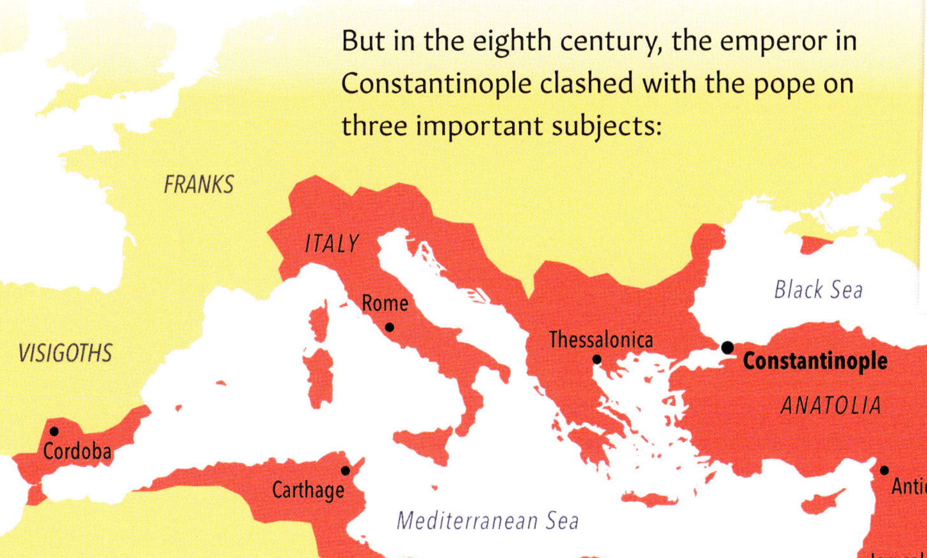

1. **Taxation:** The emperor wanted more in taxes than the pope and the people of Italy wanted to pay to someone so far away.
2. **Iconoclasm:** The emperor banned the veneration of religious images, which was unacceptable to the pope.
3. **Protection:** The people of Italy (the pope included) felt that the emperor wasn't supporting them enough or providing them enough protection from attacks.

The Donation of Pepin

When the Lombards threatened to invade Rome, Pope Stephen II (752–757) asked for help from Pepin the Short, the Frankish ruler, instead of from the Byzantine Emperor, who had traditionally been the one to protect Rome. Pepin agreed and sent troops not only to protect Rome but to recapture other territories the Lombards had already conquered.

He then gave the pope the right to rule over these territories. This is known as the Donation of Pepin. Afterward, other rulers also ceded land to the pope, who became the sovereign of vast regions of Italy.

Sovereign a supreme ruler

The Pope vs. Napoleon

The Papal States stayed largely intact for the next several centuries. Then came the French Revolution.

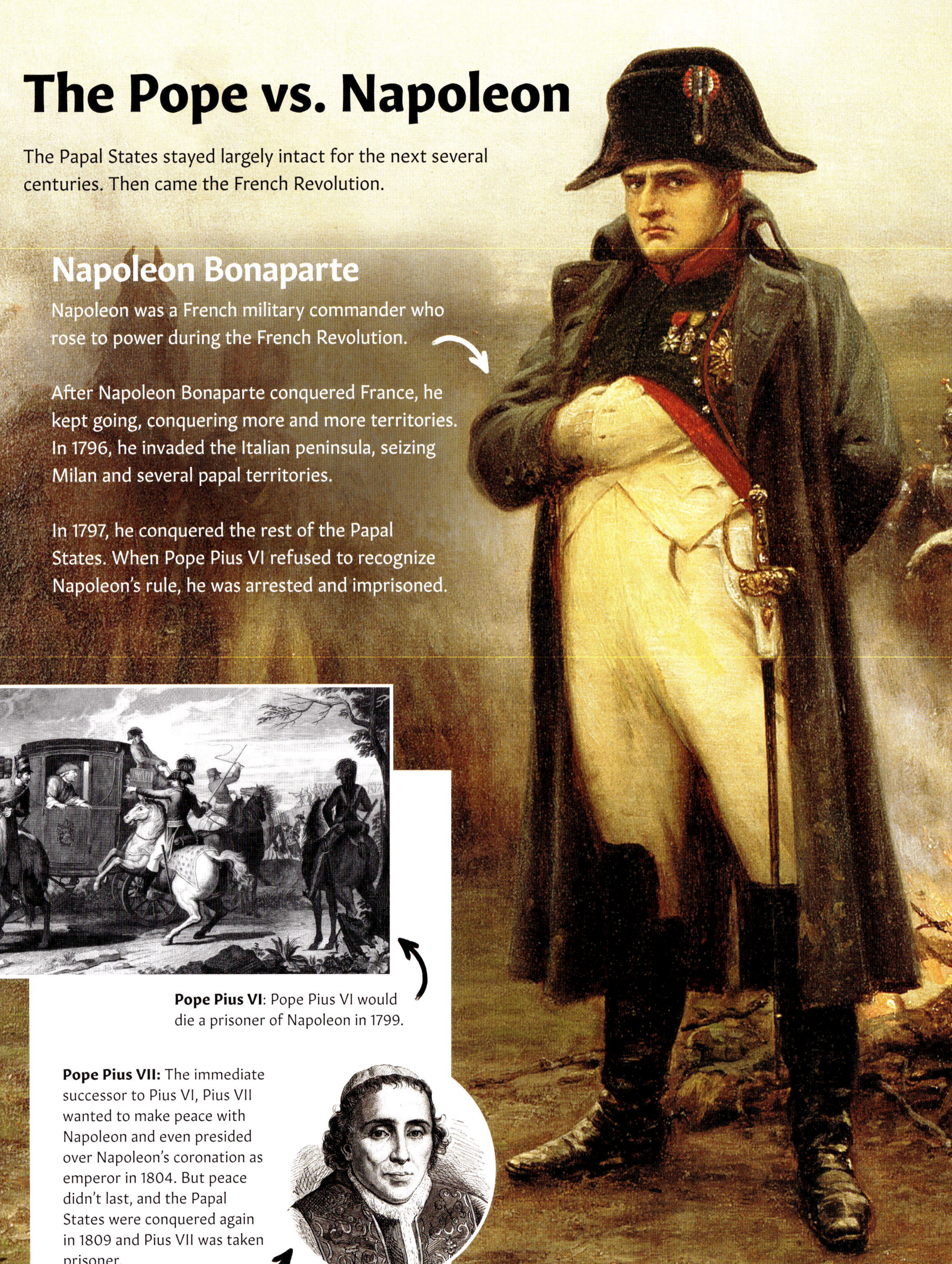

Napoleon Bonaparte

Napoleon was a French military commander who rose to power during the French Revolution.

After Napoleon Bonaparte conquered France, he kept going, conquering more and more territories. In 1796, he invaded the Italian peninsula, seizing Milan and several papal territories.

In 1797, he conquered the rest of the Papal States. When Pope Pius VI refused to recognize Napoleon's rule, he was arrested and imprisoned.

Pope Pius VI: Pope Pius VI would die a prisoner of Napoleon in 1799.

Pope Pius VII: The immediate successor to Pius VI, Pius VII wanted to make peace with Napoleon and even presided over Napoleon's coronation as emperor in 1804. But peace didn't last, and the Papal States were conquered again in 1809 and Pius VII was taken prisoner.

Italian Unification

By the late 1800s, the people of Italy decided that they had had enough of being ruled by outsiders. They wanted to be one single kingdom. But they had a problem: the Papal States cut right through the middle of the Italian peninsula.

Slowly, individual Papal States joined the new kingdom, eventually leaving only Rome itself under Papal Control. On September 20, 1870, Italian troops entered and conquered Rome. By October, the city was the new capital of the Italian Kingdom.

Pope Pius IX: Pope Pius IX (1846–1878) refused to accept this. He became a prisoner in the Vatican, unable to leave. In fact, no pope left the confines of the Vatican until 1929 with the signing of the Lateran Treaty.

The Lateran Treaty

The Lateran Treaty ended the standoff between the pope and Italy. It stated that the pope and his successors would recognize Italy as a country and Rome as its capital. Italy in return would recognize papal sovereignty over Vatican City and the full independence of the pope.

The Signing of the Lateran Treaty: The treaty was signed by the Italian dictator, Benito Mussolini, and Pietro Gasparri, Pope Pius XI's secretary of state.

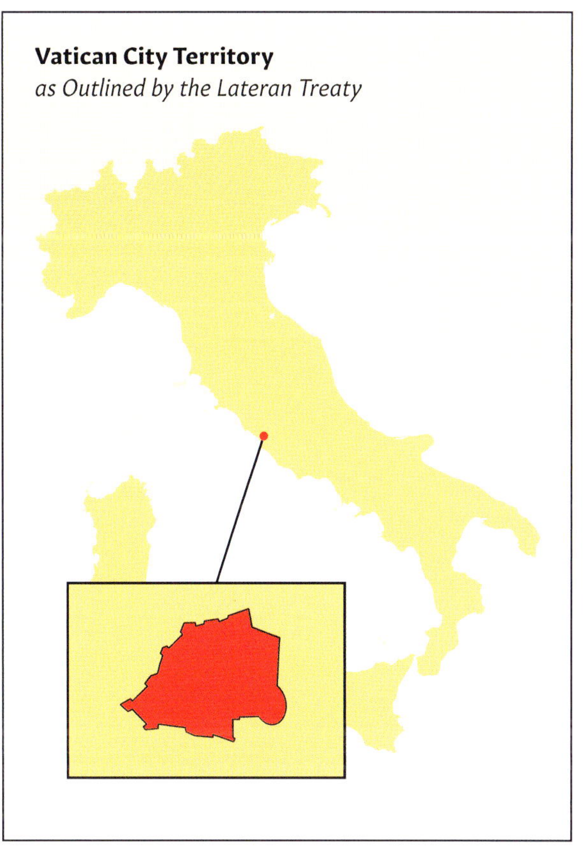

Vatican City

Vatican City was created by the Lateran Treaty. It is the residence of the pope and the seat of government for the Catholic Church.

Vatican City is a land-locked country. It is surrounded on all sides by Italy.

Holy See the name for the government of the Catholic Church, led by the pope

The Papal Flag

The papal flag has a field of gold and white. The gold symbolizes heavenly power and the white earthly power. On the white side is the papal coat of arms, which has the papal tiara and the keys to the kingdom given to Saint Peter.

The Coat of Arms

Each pope has his own coat of arms. His coat of arms, like the Vatican City flag, bears the papal tiara and the papal keys. The Holy See and Vatican City also each have their own separate coat of arms!

From left to right: Coat of Arms of Popes Benedict XVI and Francis.

Pope Leo XIV's Coat of Arms

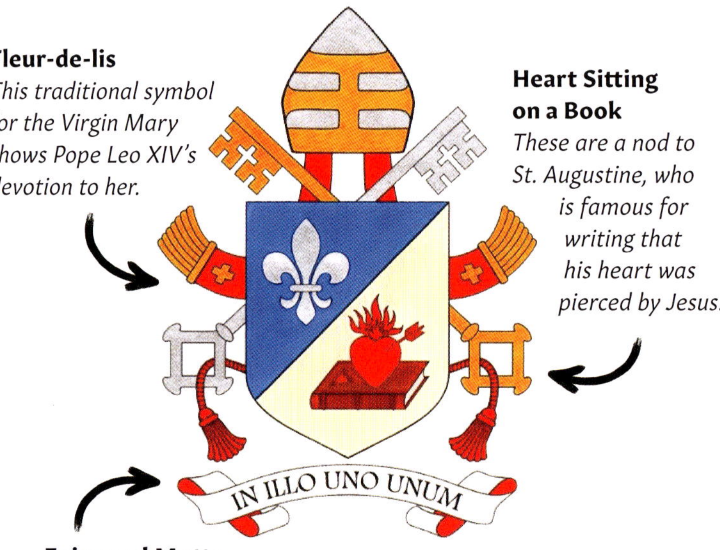

Fleur-de-lis
This traditional symbol for the Virgin Mary shows Pope Leo XIV's devotion to her.

Heart Sitting on a Book
These are a nod to St. Augustine, who is famous for writing that his heart was pierced by Jesus.

Episcopal Motto
This short phrase, Latin for "in the One we are all one", is a quote from St. Augustine. Pope Leo XIV chose it when he was consecrated a bishop.

FUN FACT

There are certain buildings and properties held by the Holy See that are located within Italian territory. These are treated in the same way that foreign embassies are.

Who Lives in Vatican City?

Fewer than one thousand people live within the walls of Vatican City, and not all of those are citizens of the country. The population varies but is mostly composed of diplomats, clergy, and the Swiss Guard.

In 2013, there were only thirteen families living in Vatican City. Citizenship of Vatican City is unlike that of many countries in the world. It is granted only to those who are working in service of the Holy See, and usually ends when that service does. Citizenship is also extended to spouses and children.

Do You Need a Passport?

No passports are needed to enter Vatican City, but certain parts of Vatican City are off-limits to tourists.

Vatican City

Official Name:
State of the Vatican City

Official Languages:
Latin and Italian

Population:
< 1,000 people

Size:
< 1 square mile

Important Places in Vatican City

Within Vatican City there are many important sites.

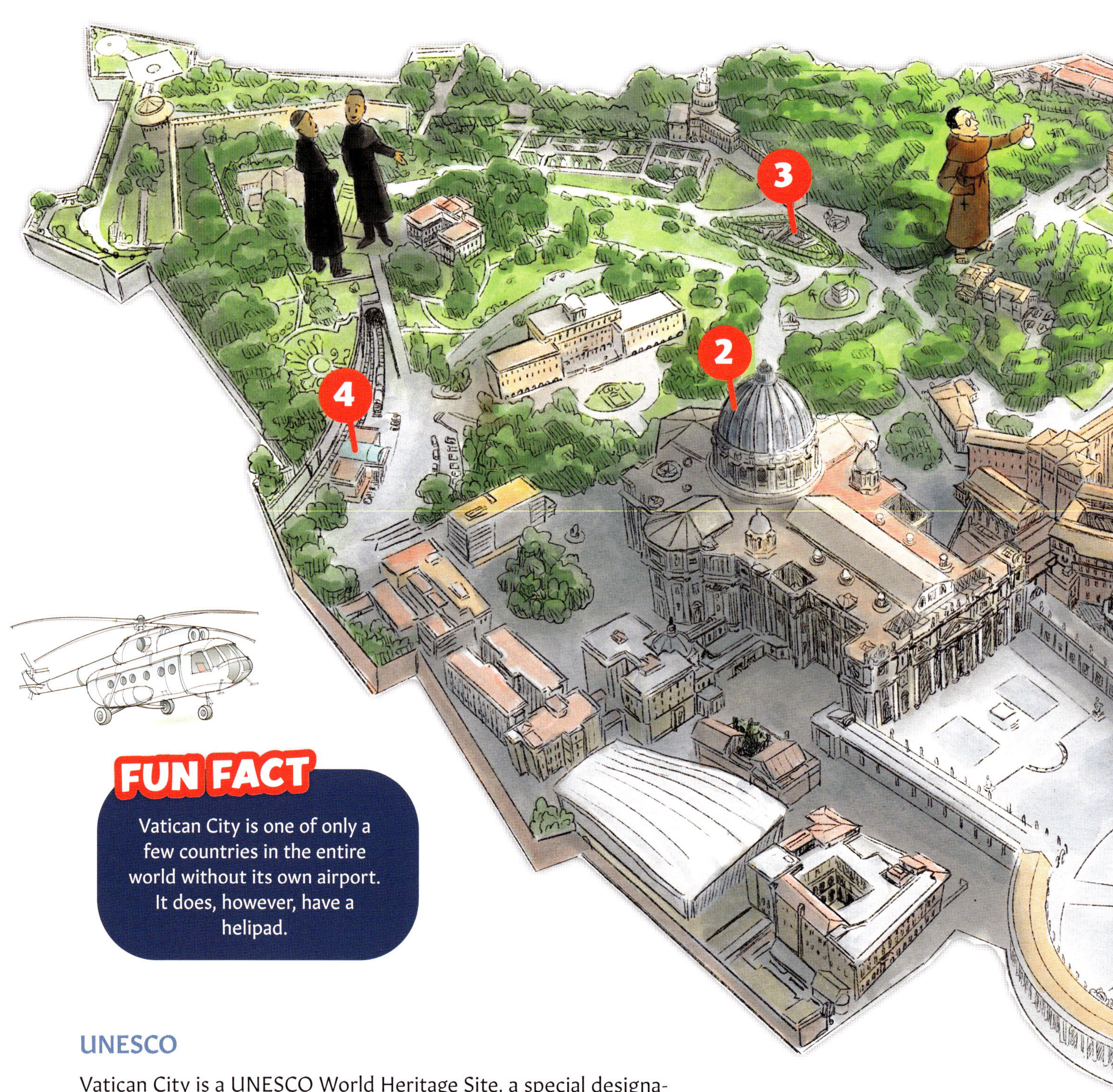

FUN FACT

Vatican City is one of only a few countries in the entire world without its own airport. It does, however, have a helipad.

UNESCO

Vatican City is a UNESCO World Heritage Site, a special designation given to places of particular cultural, political, or scientific importance in human history. Vatican City is recognized as one of the most important places in all of Christendom.

The Obelisk

One of the most unusual landmarks in Vatican City is an Egyptian obelisk that stands in Saint Peter's Square. It was brought to Rome by Emperor Caligula. It originally stood at the site of the Roman Circus, which became the location of martyrdom for many early Christians, including, according to tradition, Saint Peter.

Saint Peter's Basilica

Arguably one of the most recognizable and important places in all of Catholicism, Saint Peter's Basilica was built over the tomb of Saint Peter. The square in front of the basilica is where the pope gives his public audiences.

3 The Vatican Gardens

The Vatican Gardens are not your typical garden. Dating back to medieval times when Pope Nicholas III created an orchard, a meadow, and a garden, these grounds can only be entered on a guided tour.

A rectangular labyrinth was added to the garden in the sixteenth century.

4 The Vatican Railway Station

The Vatican boasts the world's shortest national railway. It's only 330 yards long (less than three football fields). It's mostly used for freight and connects with the Italian rail system.

5 The Vatican Museums

One of the most important museums in the world, the Vatican Museums hold more than seventy thousand works, including important pieces from Renaissance masters. Only about twenty thousand of those are on display at a time — still a staggering number! Millions of people visit each year.

The Hall of Busts is one of fifty-four Galleries in the Pio Clementino Museum containing Greek and Roman Sculptures.

7 The Secret Archives

The Secret Archives of the Vatican aren't really secret. The word comes from the Latin word *secretum*, which means private. They hold the private papers of the popes (more than thirty thousand documents) and include fascinating pieces of history like a letter from Mary, Queen of Scots, to Pope Sixtus V, begging him to save her life Mary. He did not intervene, and she was beheaded by her cousin Queen Elizabeth.

6 The Apostolic Library

The Apostolic Library at the Vatican contains one of the largest collections of ancient and medieval manuscripts in the world, as well as millions of other treasures, including maps, coins, engravings, and drawings.

The Swiss Guard

For hundreds of years, the pope has been protected by an armed division known as the Pontifical Swiss Guard.

Requirements

Swiss Guards must be unmarried Catholic men with Swiss citizenship who are between eighteen and thirty years of age and have completed basic training with the Swiss armed forces.

What Do They Do?

The job of the Swiss Guard is to protect the pope. Though they fulfill many ceremonial guard services in the Vatican, they are also fully trained members of the military.

Why the Swiss?

Guardsmen from Switzerland have been helping to protect the pope since 1506, but during the Sack of Rome in 1527, they were instrumental in saving the pope's life.

When the Holy Roman Emperor Charles V decided to capture the city of Rome, the Swiss Guard sprang into action. On May 6, 1527, 147 Swiss Guards took up position outside Saint Peter's Basilica against a force of twenty thousand. They fought to the death while the remaining 42 Swiss Guards guided the pope to safety and allowed him to escape unharmed. This heroism and willingness to give their lives for the pope earned them a special place in the Vatican.

The Uniform of the Swiss Guard

The yellow, red, and blue gala uniform of the Swiss Guard is one of the most recognizable throughout the world.

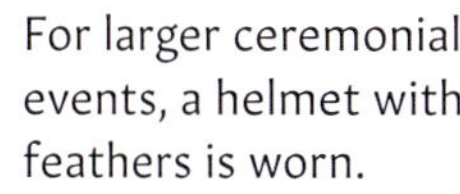

For larger ceremonial events, a helmet with feathers is worn.

The halberd is the traditional staff-like weapon carried by the Swiss Guard.

Headgear: For daily duties, the Swiss Guard wears a black beret. For larger ceremonial events, a helmet with feathers is worn.

The harnish is the seventeenth century armor worn over the uniform.

While on night guard duties or during training exercises, the Swiss Guard wears this simple navy blue uniform.

FUN FACT

The full dress uniform weighs eight pounds, making it the heaviest (and most complicated) military uniform in the world.

When the pope travels abroad, members of the Swiss Guard travel with him, dressed in plain clothes.

The Oath

When entering service, members of the Swiss Guard swear an oath of loyalty during a ceremony that occurs yearly on May 6:

"I swear I will faithfully, loyally, and honorably serve the Supreme Pontiff and his legitimate successors, and I dedicate myself to them with all my strength. I assume this same commitment with regard to the Sacred College of Cardinals whenever the Apostolic See is vacant. Furthermore, I promise to the Commanding Captain and my other superiors respect, fidelity, and obedience. I swear to observe all that the honor of position demands of me."

Papal Diplomacy

Throughout the history of the Church, popes have been powerful enemies and allies to countries, kings, and empires. As both monarch of Vatican City and head of the Catholic Church, the pope has an important role to play on the world stage.

Today the Holy See maintains diplomatic relationships with more than 180 countries. Many of these began or were expanded in the last century. Countries in green have a diplomatic relationship.

FUN FACT

Vatican City does not host any foreign embassies. Because of its size, there is no space. Many embassies to the Vatican are located in Rome.

The Coronation of Charlemagne

Popes were very involved in world politics and were often important power brokers. Pope Leo III crowned Charlemagne Emperor of the Holy Roman Empire in 800.

The Holy See is not a member of the United Nations, though it does recognize all the member countries, with the exception of the People's Republic of China.

A complicated relationship

Though the relationship between England and the pope has historically been rocky since the excommunication of King Henry VIII, Queen Elizabeth II of England (monarch of the United Kingdom and head of the Anglican Church) met with five popes during her lifetime. During her reign, diplomatic relations between the two countries were normalized.

Traditionally, women have worn black gowns with black veils, a symbol of humility and piety, to meet the pope.

Certain royal women have been allowed to exercise what is known as the *privilege du blanc*, or the privilege of white, meaning they are allowed to wear white to meet the pope.

Princess Charlene of Monaco exercised the privilege du blanc *when she and her husband, Prince Albert, met with Pope Benedict XVI in 2013.*

FUN FACT

Newlyweds are also granted this permission. Women who were recently married in the Church are allowed to wear their wedding dress at the pope's Wednesday audience and receive a special blessing!

When First Lady Michelle Obama of the United States met Pope Benedict XVI with her husband, President Barack Obama, she wore a black dress and a black veil.

The Pope and the United States

The Papal States were the first country to recognize the United States as a nation after the Treaty of Paris (the agreement that officially ended the Revolutionary War).

Conspiracy?

There was a conspiracy theory that the pope was involved in plotting the assassination of Abraham Lincoln because several of the men and women who were involved were Catholic. There is no evidence that this is true.

Timeline of Diplomacy

1784

The Papal States recognized the United States as a country in 1784.

1867

Unfortunately, as the United States began to receive more and more immigrants, anti-Catholic sentiment spread, and in 1867 Congress passed a law prohibiting any future missions to the Holy See.

Though from that point on, there were no official diplomatic relations, many presidents sent personal envoys to the pope and visited the Vatican during their administrations.

1984

Official diplomatic relations began again in 1984 when William A. Wilson was confirmed as the first US Ambassador to the Holy See.

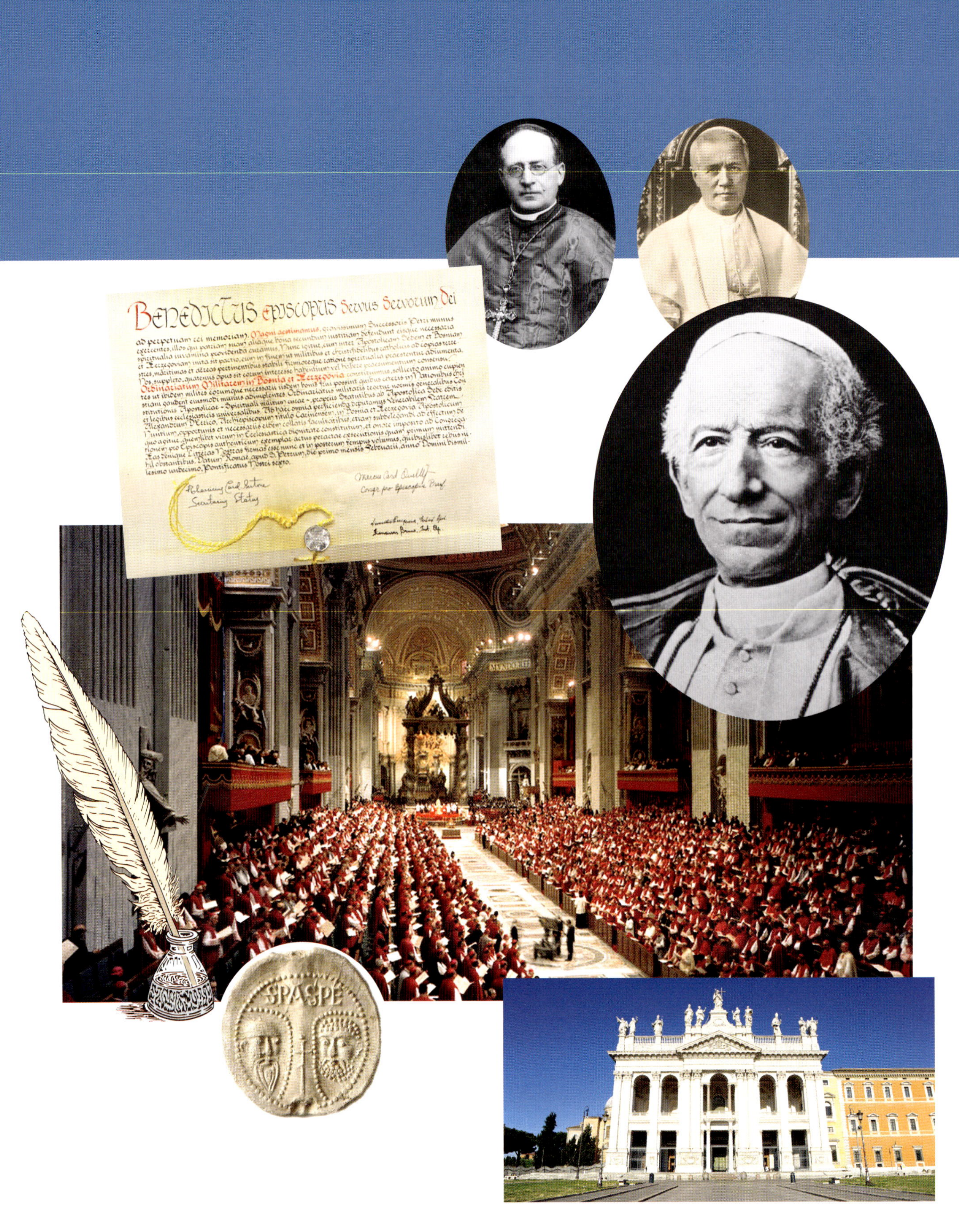
Benedictus Episcopus Servus Servorum Dei
SPA SPE

Pope as Head of Church

Papal Writings

As head of the Catholic Church, the pope does a lot of writing. He writes on topics large and small, and his writings come in many different forms.

Types of Papal Writings

- Apostolic Constitution
- Encyclical
- Apostolic Exhortation
- Apostolic Letter
- *Motu Proprio*
- Papal Bull
- Decretal Letter
- Homilies, Speeches, General Audiences

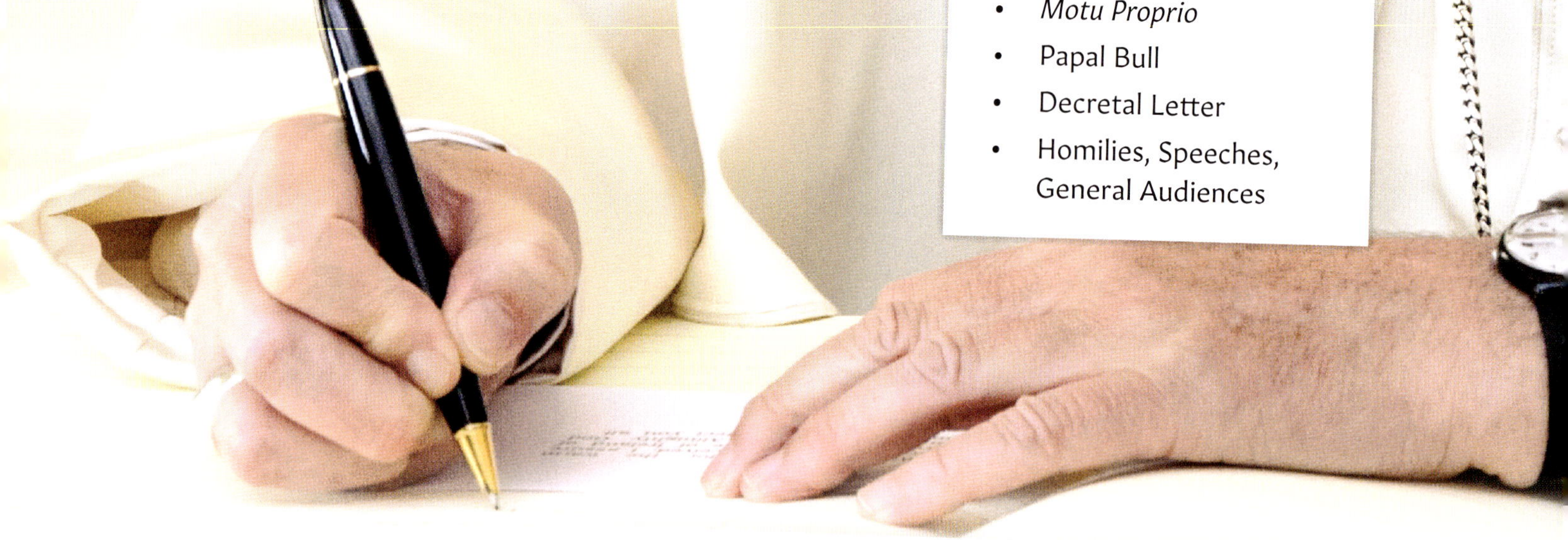

Papal writings can be either pastoral or legislative.

Pastoral concerned with giving spiritual guidance

Legislative relating to laws or the creation of them

Apostolic Constitutions

Apostolic constitutions are the most formal of all papal documents. These are often issued as bulls. They are legal documents that deal with doctrinal matters. For example, sometimes they are used to create new dioceses.

Papal Bulls

A papal bull is a formal and public decree issued by the pope. It's named after the seal that was traditionally used to authenticate it, a bulla. The pope himself signs the most solemn of the bulls. More often though, the cardinal secretary of state signs on the pope's behalf. Papal bulls are known by the first few Latin words of their text.

The style of a papal bull is always the same.

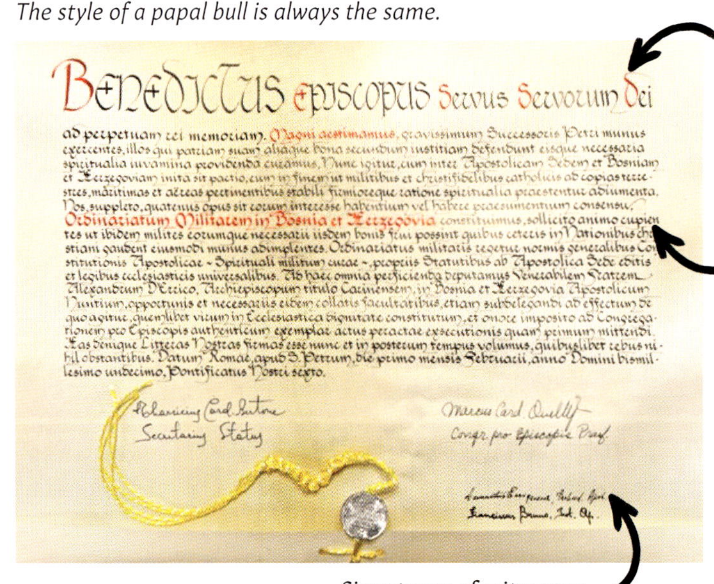

Benedictus Episcopus Servus Servorum Dei

ad perpetuam rei memoriam. Magni aestimamus, gravissimum Successoris Petri munus exercentes, illos qui patriam suam aliaque bona secundum iustitiam defendunt eisque necessaria spiritualia iuvamina providenda curamus. Nunc igitur, cum inter Apostolicam Sedem et Bosniam et Herzegoviam inita sit pactio, cum in finem ut militibus et christifidelibus catholicis ad copias terrestres, maritimas et aereas pertinentibus stabili firmioreque ratione spiritualia praestentur adiumenta, Nos, suppleto, quatenus opus sit, eorum interesse habentium vel habere praesumentium consensu, Ordinariatum Militarem in Bosnia et Herzegovia constituimus, sollicito animo cupientes ut ibidem milites eorumque necessarii iisdem bonis frui possint quibus ceteris in Nationibus christiani gaudent eiusmodi munus adimplentes. Ordinariatus militaris regetur normis generalibus Constitutionis Apostolicae «Spirituali militum curae», propriis Statutibus ab Apostolica Sede editis et legibus ecclesiasticis universalibus. Ad haec omnia perficienda deputamus Venerabilem Fratrem Alexandrum D'Errico, Archiepiscopum titulo Carinensem, in Bosnia et Herzegovia Apostolicum Nuntium, opportunis et necessariis eidem collatis facultatibus, etiam subdelegandi ad effectum de quo agitur, quemlibet virum in Ecclesiastica dignitate constitutum, et onere imposito ad Congregationem pro Episcopis authenticum exemplar actus peractae exsecutionis quam primum mittendi. Has denique Litteras Nostras firmas esse nunc et in posterum tempus volumus, quibuslibet rebus nihil obstantibus. Datum Romae, apud S. Petrum, die primo mensis Februarii, anno Domini bismillesimo undecimo, Pontificatus Nostri sexto.

First Line: pope's name, his title (*Episcopus Servus Servorum Dei*), and incipit

Body of the Text: simple; gets to the point

Closing Section: A datum tells you where and when the bull was issued.

Signatures of witnesses

Pope John XXIII signs a papal bull on Dec. 25, 1961, proclaiming that an Ecumenical Council of the Catholic Church (the Second Vatican Council) will be held in 1962.

The seal itself

The bulla, or seal, used was traditionally made of metal, often lead but occasionally gold. Today, the Church uses red ink, except in very special cases. Each bull has the faces of Saints Peter and Paul on one side and the issuing pope's name in Latin on the other.

This papal bull is one of the most famous in papal history. It was issued by Pope Leo X in 1521. In it, Pope Leo states that Martin Luther is a heretic and is excommunicated from the Church. This bull marks the beginning of the Protestant Reformation.

Excommunicated When someone is excommunicated from the Catholic Church, they are cut off from fellowship and the sacraments. It is the most severe penalty that can be given out, but it's also a call to repentance. Excommunications can be lifted through a process of reconciliation with the Church.

Motu Proprio

These are legislative letters written and signed by the pope. They deal with significant issues, but ones that aren't as serious as those covered by apostolic constitutions. They are usually brief because they deal with a specific issue at a specific time.

Motu proprio is Latin for "by one's own initiative." These documents get their names because they are written by the pope on subjects that he feels strongly about.

Encyclical

Encyclicals are the most well known of all papal writings. These long papal letters are pastoral, meaning they are written to the people of the Church to encourage, teach, and inspire.

The word *encyclical* comes from the Greek word *enkyklios* meaning circular. This name comes because the letters were meant to be widely circulated.

FUN FACT

It's the same word we get "encyclopedia" from.

Encyclical History

Originally, an encyclical (or circulating letter) was a letter sent out by a bishop to all the churches in a particular area.

Later, it became the term used for letters that the pope wrote to the bishops.

Today, encyclicals are primarily written by the pope for the entire Church. They've only become common since the papacy of Pius IX (1846–1878).

In 1740, Pope Benedict XIV wrote Ubi Primum *which is generally considered the first papal encyclical.*

In the modern era, a papal encyclical is a specific type of document. Encyclicals are pastoral in nature. Topics vary widely (everything from condemning Nazism to caring for the earth has been covered by encyclicals), but are usually need-based, meaning the pope feels that the topic is something the Church should focus on.

Pope Benedict XVI signing the encyclical Caritas in Veritate, *Rome.*

Important to note!

Encyclicals are not automatically infallible. Popes are considered to be infallible only when they are speaking *ex cathedra*, which means "from the chair of Saint Peter."

Infallible incapable of making mistakes

Encyclicals are more personal than a papal bull, but like a bull, they are always written in Latin, the language of the Church.

The name for each encyclical comes from the first few words of the text.

This is __________

by Pope ______ *which*

means ______________

in English.

Top 5 Encyclical Writers

Pope Leo XIII
between 1878 and 1902
86

Pope Pius XII
41

Pope Pius XI
33

Pope Pius X
16

Pope John Paul II
14

Other Types of Papal Writings

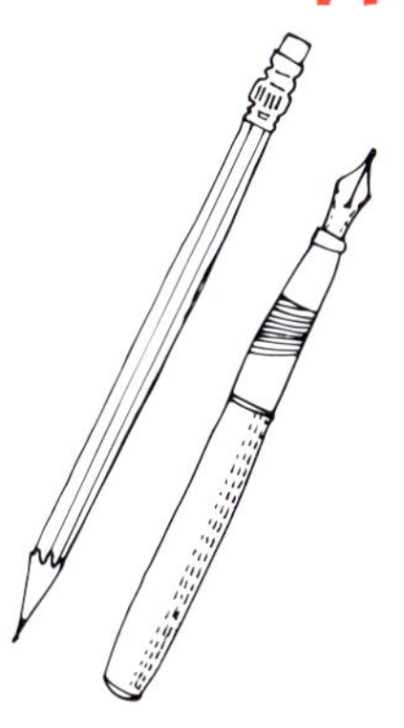

Papal Letters

These are pastoral letters. They offer counsel on a topic that is important to the pope.

Apostolic Exhortations

These are papal reflections on a specific topic that are addressed to everyone in the Church.

Apostolic Letters

These differ from encyclicals in authority and purpose and are written in response to a particular need or to a specific group of people. These are pastoral, not legislative.

Decretal Letters

These are letters that give a pontifical decision. The announcements of canonizations are often decretal letters.

Papal Infallibility

Papal infallibility is one of the most misunderstood parts of papal authority. It was defined by the First Vatican Council in 1870. It means that the Holy Spirit won't let the pope make a mistake concerning Church doctrine. Infallibility is a safeguard, not a way to create new doctrine.

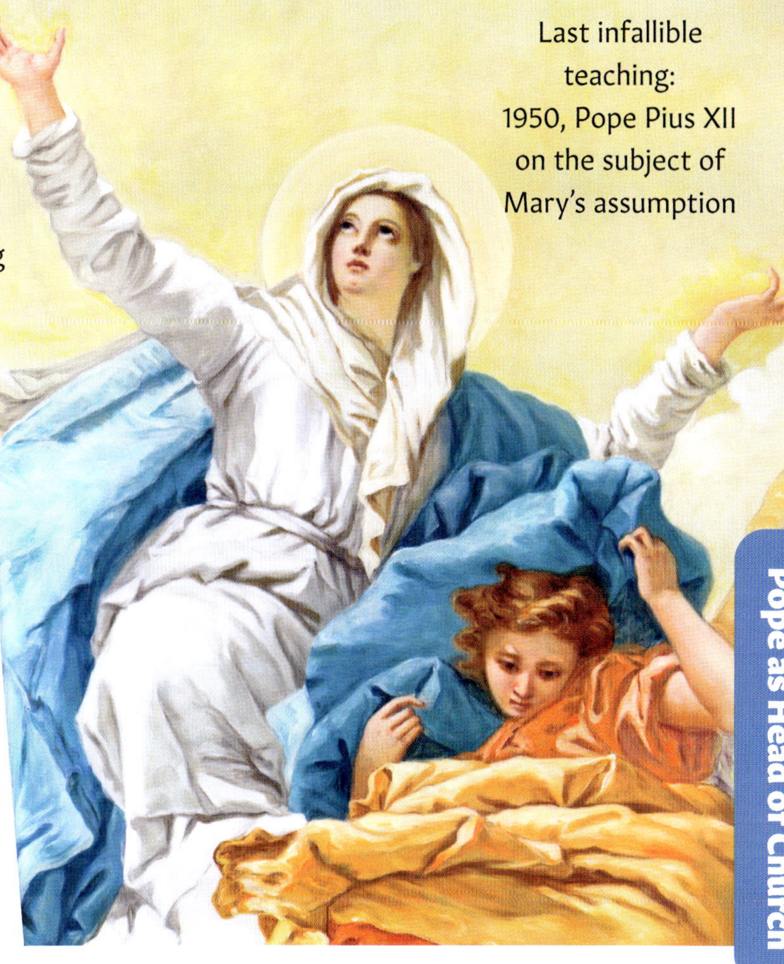

Last infallible teaching: 1950, Pope Pius XII on the subject of Mary's assumption

Infallibility requires three conditions:

The subject the pope is teaching or speaking on is a matter of faith or morals.

The pope must be teaching as supreme pastor.

The pope must say that the teaching is infallible.

Ecumenical Councils

From time to time throughout Church history, there have been large gatherings called ecumenical councils. These are meetings of the bishops of the Church, and all of them throughout the world are invited. There have been twenty-one ecumenical councils.

What Makes a Council "Ecumenical"?

An ecumenical council becomes ecumenical when the pope approves its work.

FUN FACT

The pope doesn't have to attend the council; he just gives it his stamp of approval. Especially early in the history of the Church, when travel was difficult, the pope would send a representative and then approve the council's decrees when it finished its work.

What Does an Ecumenical Council Do?

Over the centuries, councils have denounced heresies, formulated the Nicene Creed (which we still say today), and defined important tenets of the faith.

Councils can be doctrinal (having to do with Church teachings), pastoral (having to do with the spiritual life of the people of God), or both.

Heresy a belief that is contrary to Church teaching

Who Attends an Ecumenical Council?

The world's bishops, as well as other important members of the Church, are invited to ecumenical councils. Early councils always included the reigning emperor and his representatives.

Popes-to-be John Paul II and Benedict XVI both attended the Second Vatican Council.

The Twenty-One Councils

Ecumenical councils are named for their locations.

325	Nicaea I	*Pope Sylvester I*	Condemned Arianism (a heresy that denied the divinity of Christ); began writing the Nicene Creed (the statement of belief Catholics say at Mass)
381	Constantinople I	*Pope Damasus I*	Finished the Nicene Creed; condemned Macedonianism (a heresy that denied the divinity of the Holy Spirit)
431	Ephesus	*Pope Celestine I*	Defined that Mary is the *Theotokos*, or God-bearer, meaning that Mary is the Mother of God; condemned Pelagianism (a heresy that said that man can earn salvation through his own works)
451	Chalcedon	*Pope Leo the Great*	Condemned Monophysitism (a heresy that denied Jesus' human nature)
553	Constantinople II	*Pope Vigilius*	Condemned a work called "Three Chapters," which had theological errors
680	Constantinople III	*Pope Agatho*	Condemned Monothelitism (a heresy that said that Christ has only a divine will and not a human one)
787	Nicaea II	*Pope Hadrian I*	Condemned iconoclasm (a heresy that said that using images was idolatry)
869	Constantinople IV	*Pope Hadrian II*	Ended the Photian Schism, which was a break between the pope and the patriarch of Constantinople
1123	Lateran I	*Pope Callistus II*	Settled a conflict between the pope and Emperor Henry V.

1139	**Lateran II**	*Pope Innocent II*	Ended a papal schism; decreed that priests could not be married
1179	**Lateran III**	*Pope Alexander III*	Said that papal elections require a vote by at least two-thirds of the cardinals; condemned Albigensianism (a heresy that taught, among other things, that matter is evil)
1215	**Lateran IV**	*Pope Innocent III*	Required that Catholics receive the Eucharist and penance at least once a year; used the word *transubstantiation* to explain the Real Presence
1245	**Lyons I**	*Pope Innocent IV*	Excommunicated and deposed Emperor Frederick II for heresy and crimes against the Church (Frederick was holding Rome under siege at the time)
1274	**Lyons II**	*Pope Gregory X*	Tried to reunite the Eastern and Western Churches and end the East/West Schism; discussed a crusade to conquer the Holy Land

The East/West Schism

In 1054, the Greek Church broke from the Catholic Church over the addition of the filioque *clause in the Nicene Creed. This was the part of the Creed that says that the Holy Spirit proceeds from the Father and the Son. This led to the creation of the Eastern Orthodox Church, which holds that the Holy Spirit proceeds only from the Father.*

FUN FACT

Zelus fidei, the decree that was approved after the Second Council of Lyon, also contained a section that excommunicated pirates and corsairs.

The Knights Templar was a military order that was created to protect pilgrims traveling to the Holy Land.

1311	**Vienne**	*Pope Clement V*	Dissolved the Knights Templar and called them heretics (this was done under pressure by King Phillip IV of France, who wanted their wealth and lands)
1414	**Constance**	*Pope Gregory XII*	During this time there were three rival popes. During the council, two of them were deposed, and one (Gregory XII) abdicated after convening the council. The council then elected Pope Martin V.

Dates	Council	Popes	Outcome
1438–1443	Florence		Reaffirmed papal primacy; tried unsuccessfully to reunite with some of the Eastern Churches.
1512–1517	Lateran V	*Popes Julius II and Leo X*	Decreed the immortality of the soul; declared that the pope is superior in authority to Church councils

This was the first council to span multiple popes.

Dates	Council	Popes	Outcome
1545–1549, 1551–1552, 1562–1563	Trent	*Popes Paul III, Julius III, Pius IV*	Responded to the Protestant Reformation; clarified doctrines that the Protestants argued against and instituted reforms within the Church
1869–1870	Vatican I	*Pope Pius IX*	Defined papal infallibility; declared the pope has full jurisdiction over the whole Church and can speak to the whole Church

This council was split into three parts.

The First Vatican Council was cut short by war and the occupation of Rome. It was suspended and never formally concluded.

Dates	Council	Popes	Outcome
1962–1965	Vatican II	*Popes John XXIII and Paul VI*	Authorized Mass in languages other than Latin; focused on updating the Church, specifically how she relates to the modern world

The Council that Shocked the World

When Pope John XXIII announced that he was calling a new ecumenical council, it was a surprise to everyone, even to the cardinals who were meeting with him at the time. There hadn't been a Church council in almost a hundred years.

Bishop of Rome

In addition to being the head of the worldwide Catholic Church, the pope is also a bishop — the Bishop of Rome. The Diocese of Rome is about 340 square miles, but interestingly not all of the city of Rome is part of the Roman diocese. The city got so big that it outgrew the boundaries of the diocese. Parts of Rome are in the Dioceses of Ostia and Porto-Santa Rufina.

The Cathedral

The cathedral of the Diocese of Rome is Saint John Lateran. It is considered to be the Mother Church of all Catholics in the world.

FUN FACT

During World War II, the Lateran cathedral was used by Pope Pius XII as a safe haven from the Nazis for Jews and other refugees.

Every cathedral has a throne for the bishop: the cathedra. The throne in Saint John Lateran is the papal throne.

The Basilica of Saint John Lateran has its own feast day in the calendar of the Church. On November 9 of each year, the Church celebrates the dedication of the church.

It's a Mouthful!

Full Name: Archbasilica Cathedral of the Most Holy Savior and of Saints John the Baptist and John the Evangelist in the Lateran

Who Helps the Pope?

The pope is a busy man with many responsibilities, so two vicars general help him take care of the Diocese of Rome. Each has a territory under his care.

Vicar General the representative of the bishop in matters of administration

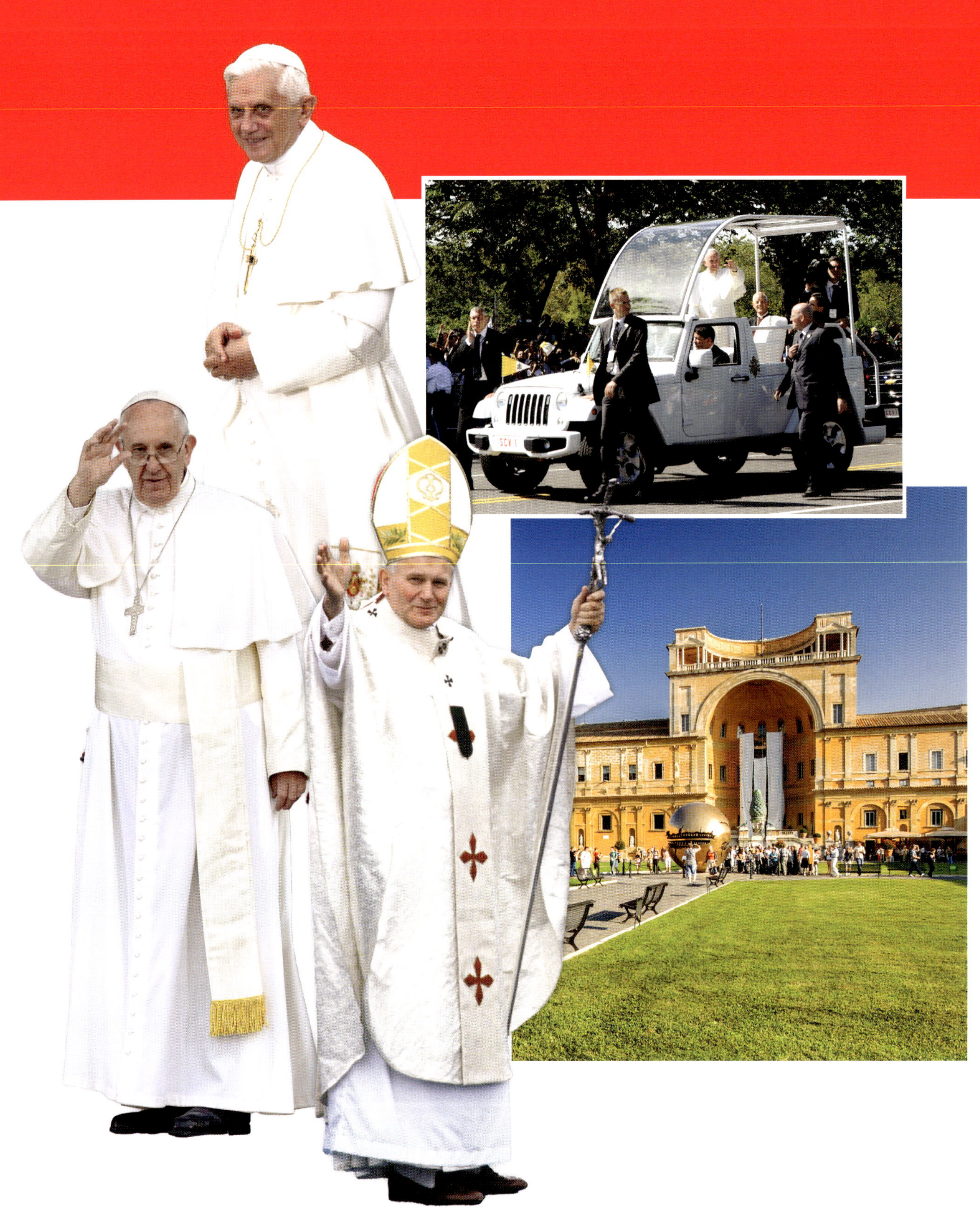
SCV 1

Papal Daily Life

What Does the Pope Do All Day?

Naturally, as both head of state and head of Church, the pope is a very busy man. He has many responsibilities, and his schedule is very full.

The cornerstone of the pope's day is prayer and the celebration of Mass. Each day begins with prayer, and if there is not a public Mass scheduled, the pope celebrates Mass in his own private chapel.

In addition to prayer, the pope spends much of his time in meetings. He meets with bishops, cardinals, and Vatican officials to discuss Church business.

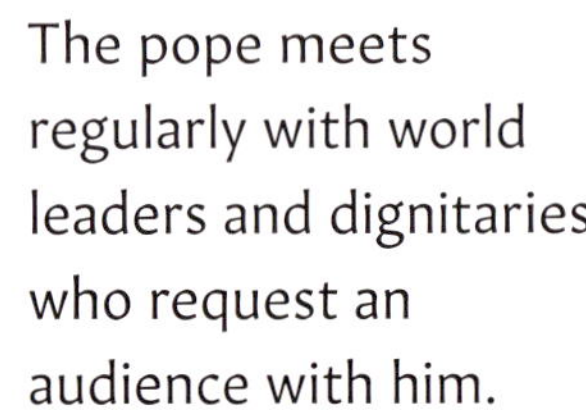

The pope meets regularly with world leaders and dignitaries who request an audience with him.

Sometimes the pope will meet with movie stars and musicians.

When the pope is in Rome, he holds public audiences on Wednesdays. These are free and open to the public, though tickets are required.

The pope writes and reviews important Church documents including letters and encyclicals.

In Rome and abroad, the pope gives many speeches and homilies on a variety of topics.

Papal Vacations?

Even the pope needs a break sometimes. For rest and relaxation, most popes go to Castel Gandolfo. It's a ten-minute helicopter ride from the Vatican, though there's also a train that runs directly there!

The papal palace of Castel Gandolfo has been used by popes for centuries as a summer home. It sits on a lake and is surrounded by beautiful gardens. Pope John Paul II even put in a swimming pool during his papacy.

Dress Like a Pope

How can you tell it's the pope? Look at his outfit! Though for much of history the pope dressed in red, for the last several centuries the pope has worn white (with a couple of fun red accessories!).

Zucchetto: a skull cap. The pope wears white. Bishops and cardinals also wear zucchettos, but theirs are purple and red, respectively.

FUN FACT

The word *zucchetto* comes from the Italian word for little pumpkin.

Ordinary Dress

For everyday occasions, you'll find the pope dressed like this.

Pellegrina: a short open cape that reaches to the elbows. The pope's pellegrina is entirely white.

Ferula: a staff carried by the pope symbolizing his role as shepherd. It has a cross at the top. Each pope has a unique ferula.

Pectoral Cross: a cross worn on the chest, hanging from the neck by a rope or chain

Cassock: the robe traditionally worn by priests, bishops, and, of course, the pope

Fascia: a fringed sash worn above the waist with the ends hanging down on the left side

Sometimes the Vatican gets chilly! Here's Pope Benedict XVI wearing a fur-lined mozzetta, which is a different type of cape worn by the pope. This one is buttoned up in the front.

Liturgical Dress

When celebrating Mass, the pope will wear the papal vestments.

The pallium is a special vestment worn only by the pope. It's worn over his chasuble.

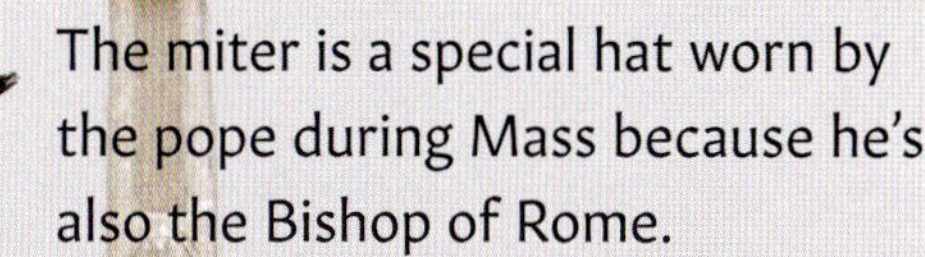

The miter is a special hat worn by the pope during Mass because he's also the Bishop of Rome.

FUN FACT

The miter is worn only at six points during Mass: the entrance and farewell processionals, the readings, the homily, while distributing the Eucharist, and during the final blessing. When it's not being worn, a miter can fold flat.

Papal Shoes

Though he isn't obligated to wear red shoes, many popes have followed this tradition. In the Church, the color red symbolizes the Blood of Christ and also the descent of the Holy Spirit in tongues of fire at Pentecost.

Even when keeping to the color red, each pope has his own sense of style. Pope Benedict XVI enjoyed wearing loafers, while Pope Pius VII preferred his to lace up.

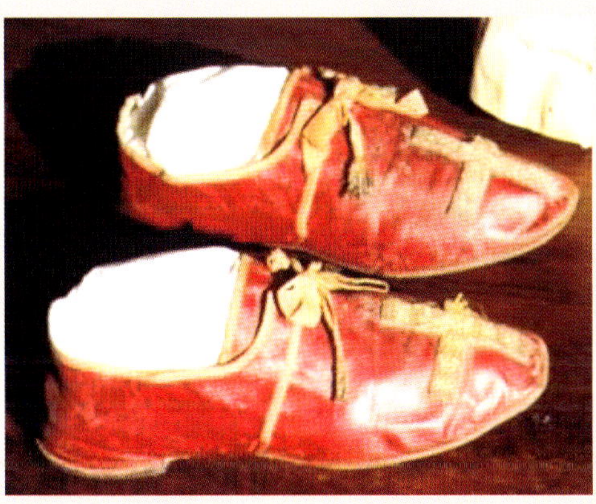

Once upon a time, the pope (like many kings and noblemen) wore slippers when inside. The pope's were, like his outdoor shoes, red. Papal slippers were elaborate — made of silk or satin, often adorned with rubies and embroidered with large gold crosses.

Papal Travel

Historically, the pope did not often leave Rome, at least not voluntarily. There were several popes who were driven out of Rome and forced to live in exile or kidnapped and taken out of the city.

Top 5 Most Visited Countries

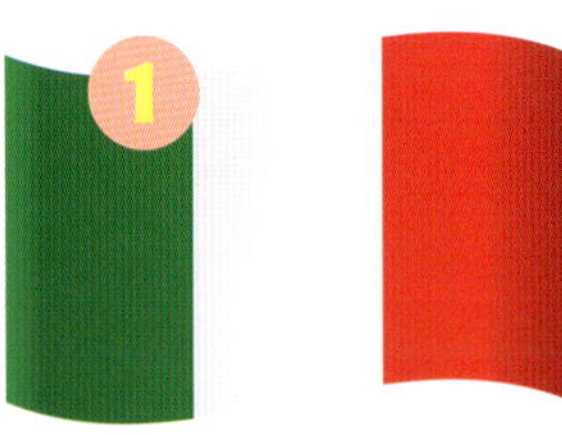

Italy: With Vatican City being in Italy, popes have been visiting the country for all 2,000+ years of the papacy. Just about every pope!

Poland: twelve visits total. Pope John Paul II, the first Polish pope, made nine visits to Poland during his papacy.

France: eleven visits, not including popes who lived in France. This country has a long history with the papacy, especially with some popes living in France during the Avignon Papacy.

United States of America: ten visits. Since the beginning of papal air travel, popes have been visiting the United States of America more, making it the fourth most visited country.

Brazil: five visits. Brazil has the world's largest Catholic population, making it an important destination for papal visits.

Papal Visit Honorable Mentions: Spain, Mexico, Portugal, and Germany

In the modern age, travel has become much easier, and popes have taken advantage of new technology to allow them to travel across the globe.

Countries Visited by

Pope Paul VI was the first pope to fly on an airplane. On January 4, 1964, he flew to the Holy Land. He traveled so much that he became known as the Pilgrim Pope, going to six continents before he died.

Pope Paul VI

19

Pope John Paul II

129

Pope Benedict XVI

25

Pope Francis

66

Pope Leo XIV

1 ***and counting!***

Pope Stephen II was the first pope to cross the Alps. He did this in 752.

FUN FACT

No pope has ever visited Antarctica.

Key

Top 5 Most Visited Countries

Countries popes have come from

The Popemobile

"Popemobile" is the nickname for a vehicle that carries the pope. In reality, there are many popemobiles, each designed to make the pope visible to crowds while also keeping him safe. Depending on the location and situation, a popemobile may be an open-air car or enclosed in bulletproof glass.

Before the Popemobile

Used until 1978, the *sedia gestatoria* was a portable papal throne. It was carried on the shoulders of twelve men and was designed to make the pope more visible to the crowds hoping to catch a glimpse of him.

The First Popemobile

Nürburg 460 by Mercedes

This Mercedes Benz was gifted to Pope Pius XI in 1930 by the car company. Called by Vatican insiders "The Rome Car," it had silk carpets and a dove motif on the ceiling.

FSC Star 660 Popemobile

This extra-large popemobile was used on Pope John Paul II's trip to Poland in 1979.

Pope John Paul II disliked the term "popemobile" so much that he asked people to stop using it. But the "undignified" term stuck around and is even used today by the Church.

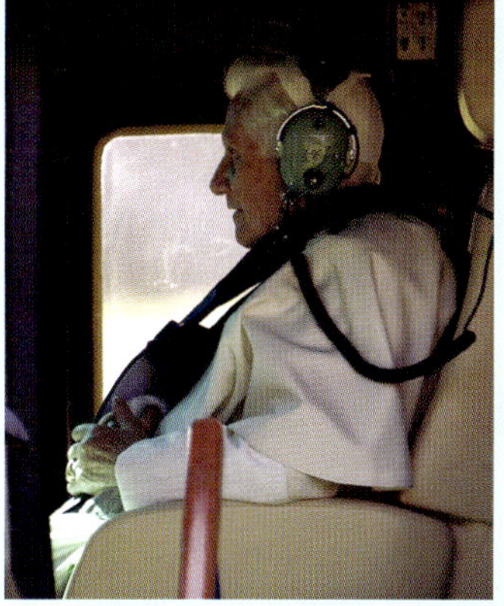

Pope Benedict never learned to drive a car, but he did learn to pilot the papal helicopter. With this pilot's license, he would fly from the Vatican to Castel Gandolfo for his summer vacation.

Shepherd One

The papal equivalent of Air Force One, Shepherd One is the name given to the plane the pope flies on. There is no single Shepherd One plane, however. The Vatican does not own any airplanes and usually charters a plane for papal travel.

One of Pope Francis's final wishes after his death was that the popemobile used during his 2014 visit to Bethlehem be refitted as a mobile health clinic to serve the children of war-torn Gaza.

Fiat Campagnola

This is the popemobile that Pope John Paul II was riding in when he was shot. His assassination attempt is the reason many popemobiles since have included bulletproof glass.

Pope Francis in a Jeep popemobile in Washington, D.C., in September 2015.

Does the Pope Have a Driver's License?

Though the pope doesn't usually drive himself, some popes, including Pope Francis, have had driver's licenses.

The Pope's License Plate

The license plate of the popemobile reads SCV1. The letters are an abbreviation of *Status Civitatis Vaticanae*, which is Latin for "Vatican City State."

The Papal Apartments

The official residence of the pope, when he is in Vatican City, is the apostolic palace, located adjacent to Saint Peter's Basilica. In addition to various sets of papal apartments, the building contains offices, chapels, libraries, and museums.

Until 1870, the Quirinal Palace was the pope's official residence. It's now the home of the president of the Italian Republic.

Each Sunday at noon, the pope appears at the window of the papal apartment to give a weekly address. It is usually a short homily on the Sunday reading. He then prays the Angelus and greets the pilgrims who wait in Saint Peter's Square. The Angelus address is given in Italian but is later translated into English, Spanish, Portuguese, French, German, and Arabic. The prayers themselves are recited in Latin.

Can People Visit the Papal Apartments?

While the current papal apartments are not open to visitors, suites of rooms used by past popes are.

The Sistine Chapel

The Sistine Chapel, which was built in 1473, is the most famous of the papal chapels at the apostolic palace. Its walls and ceilings are decorated by enormous frescoes by Botticelli, Michelangelo, and other famous Renaissance artists.

Here's a close up of one of the walls in the ornate Borgia apartments.

The Borgia Apartments

These were the rooms of Pope Alexander VI, an infamous pope so disliked by the pope who came after him (Pope Julius II) that he refused to live there. The rooms were shut off and the frescoes were covered with black cloth.

Does the Pope Have to Live There?

No. While most popes have chosen to live in the papal apartments, it is not required. When he was elected pope, Pope Francis decided to stay in his smaller home in the Domus Sanctae Marthae, a guest house for clergy in Vatican City.

Devout Catholics, tourists, and art students from around the world flock to this particular room to see the famous School of Athens, pictured here.

The Raphael Rooms

When Pope Julius II was elected, he decided he didn't like the rooms that his predecessor had used. So he commissioned Raphael to paint frescoes (over ones that already existed) on the walls of a different set of rooms that would become his apartments. Today these rooms are known as the Raphael Rooms and are some of the most popular parts of the Vatican Museums.

Are the Papal Apartments Really an Apartment?

Yes and no. The papal apartments are a collection of rooms that the pope lives in, but are much larger than what most people think of when they hear the word "apartment."

In addition to a living room, dining room, kitchen, and the pope's bedroom, the papal apartments include a private study, a library, a rooftop garden, a medical suite (in case the pope needs to have emergency surgery), and rooms for the pope's staff.

Pope Benedict XVI renovated the papal apartments in 2005, building a new library to house his collection of more than 20,000 books.

Papal Pets

Though today no pets (other than service animals) are allowed inside Vatican City, popes throughout the centuries have enjoyed having animal companions both large and small.

Cortile de Belvedere

For more than seven hundred years, the papal gardens were home to menageries: collections of exotic animals including leopards, ostriches, rhinos, apes, and birds. In addition to entertaining the pope, the animals were a show of papal power and riches.

World leaders gave rare animals to the pope to solidify their relationships with the Holy See. When Pope Leo X was elected in 1513, the king of Portugal sent him an elephant named Hanno. Hanno became so popular that the pope established visiting hours for tourists to come and see him perform tricks. Tragically, Hanno became sick after two years in Rome. Pope Leo, who loved him dearly, had him buried in the papal gardens. His bones were discovered by surprised construction workers in 1962.

Some popes have preferred more usual pets. Pope Benedict XVI was sometimes called "the cat whisperer" because of his love of feline companions. He'd often stop on the street to pet the stray cats he saw.

Pope Pius XII was so well known for his love of animals that when a gardener found a finch with a hurt wing, he brought the bird right to the pope, who nursed her back to health and named her Gretel. Gretel was his constant companion, often seen perched on his shoulder. She even ate dinner with the pope!

HELLO
MY NAME IS
LEO·XIII· PONT. MAX.

Becoming Pope

The Death of a Pope

What happens when the pope dies? The cardinal camerlengo has the job of verifying that the pope is dead. He does this by calling his name three times in front of witnesses. He then takes the Ring of the Fisherman.

Who Is the Cardinal Camerlengo?

The cardinal camerlengo is an office within the papal household. He is in charge of the property and revenues of the Holy See. When the pope dies, he ensures that the ordinary activities of the Church keep going.

Why Take the Pope's Ring?

The Ring of the Fisherman is the papal signet ring. It was traditionally used to seal papal documents and letters. Traditionally, the papal ring was destroyed after the pope died to prevent it from being stolen and used to create fake Church documents.

Today, two deep gashes in the shape of a cross are placed on the papal ring, signifying the end of a pope's reign.

You can see Pope Leo XIII's name around the top of the ring with the image of Peter fishing below. This is to show that the popes are meant to be fishers of men.

The *Sede Vacante*

This is the time between when a pope dies and a new pope is named. During this time, the College of Cardinals takes over control of running the Church.

What Happens during the *Sede Vacante?*

- Four to six days after his death, the pope is buried.
- All cardinals under the age of eighty travel to Rome for the upcoming election of the new pope.
- Fifteen days after the pope's death, the conclave is called.

College of Cardinals The group of men who have been designated to the rank of cardinal in the Catholic Church. Like the bird that shares their name, cardinals can be known by their red clothes. The color red symbolizes that they are the pope's closest advisors and are ready to shed their blood for the Church.

Can a Pope Resign?

Yes. It is permissible for a pope to resign, though there have only been a few cases in history when this has happened.

When a pope resigns, it must be done freely of his own will, but because he is the head of the Church, he doesn't actually turn in his resignation to anyone in particular.

Pope Benedict XVI resigned the papacy on February 28, 2013. Three weeks earlier he had announced his plan to resign due to his age and failing health. He was the first pope in 600 years to resign.

After his resignation, Pope Benedict XVI took on the title of pope emeritus and lived quietly in the Vatican.

How Is a Pope Chosen?

When the pope dies (or resigns), a new pope must be chosen to succeed him.

The Papal Conclave

The conclave is a meeting of all of the cardinals under the age of eighty around the world who have gathered to elect a new pope. They follow many rules and procedures dating back centuries.

Papabile An Italian word used to describe a man who is considered to be a potential future pope. It literally means pope-able, or able to be pope.

Don't Go Anywhere!

Cardinals are not allowed to leave the Sistine Chapel except to go to the bathroom or if they are sick. If a cardinal leaves for any other reason during the conclave, he is not allowed back in.

How Does It Work?

The cardinals gather together in the Sistine Chapel, where they are read the rules of the conclave.

There are strict rules about who is allowed into the chapel during the conclave.

- Priests may hear confessions.
- There are doctors and nurses available if someone gets sick.
- A few staff are allowed in to prepare meals and handle clean up.
- Everyone is sworn to secrecy. There's even the threat of immediate excommunication if someone blabs.

It takes a two-thirds majority of votes to elect a new pope. If no pope is elected, the voting continues. There are two votes in the morning and two in the afternoon each day.

It's All a Secret!

Papal elections are held by secret ballots. Each cardinal has a vote, and before he turns in his ballot, he swears an oath that the name he wrote down is the person he thinks would be best for the job.

I elect as Supreme Pontiff

The Oath

Testor Christum Dominum, qui me iudicaturus est, me eum eligere, quem secundum Deum iudico eligi debere.

I call as my witness Christ the Lord, who will be my judge, that my vote is given to the one who before God I think should be elected

Black Smoke or White Smoke?

To make sure that no one finds out who voted for whom or what the tallies were, papal ballots are burned after they are counted.

Black smoke is made using potassium perchlorate, anthracene, and sulfur.

White smoke is made using potassium chlorate, lactose, and rosin (a resin often used on violin bows).

It's All Chemistry!

To make the smoke different colors, the Vatican adds chemicals to the ballots as they are being burned.

Catholics from around the world watch the specially erected chimney for signs of whether a vote was successful. If the vote did not result in a pope's election, the smoke from the burned ballots will be black, but if a new pope was elected, the smoke will be white.

What Happens Next?

The Room of Tears

After being elected pope and accepting the office, the new pope announces his papal name. He is greeted by the cardinals, who offer their allegiance, then he goes into the Room of Tears.

Three sets of papal robes are laid out here at the beginning of the conclave, in sizes small, medium, and large, ready for whomever is elected.

A small room off to the side of the Sistine Chapel, this is where the newly elected pope gets dressed.

The room gets its name because of the many tears the newly elected popes have shed here over the years as they spend a few minutes in private getting used to their new role.

Habemus Papam

These words, Latin for "We have a pope!" are called out from the balcony at Saint Peter's after the pope's election.

Annuntio vobis gaudium magnum; *habemus Papam:*	I announce to you a great joy; we have a pope:
Eminentissimum ac Reverendissimum Dominum, *Dominum* [first name] *Sanctae Romanae Ecclesiae Cardinalem* [surname] *qui sibi nomen imposuit* [papal name].	The most eminent and most reverend lord, Lord [first name] Cardinal of the Holy Roman Church [surname] who has taken the name [papal name].

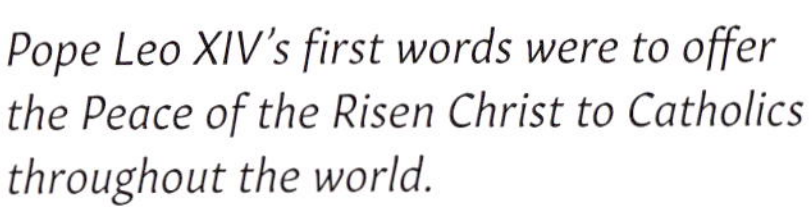

Pope Leo XIV's first words were to offer the Peace of the Risen Christ to Catholics throughout the world.

What's in a Name?

Papal Names Throughout the Ages

For many centuries, popes simply kept the names they were given at birth. But papal name changes have become the norm. How did that happen?

Name Changes Are Biblical

A change in name can be a sign of a major life change. Abram became Abraham. Jacob became Israel. Simon was renamed Peter. Saul became Paul. By taking a new name, the pope signals that he is ready to embark on a new stage of life and a new mission from God.

Name Changes Are Regal

In addition to his role as the Bishop of Rome and leader of the Catholic Church, the pope is also a monarch. When a queen or a king is crowned, they take what is known as a regnal name. This name is the name that will be used during their reign, and is sometimes different from their first name.

Can a Pope Still Use His Old Name?

Yes. Even though his new name will be used in official settings for the rest of his life, his old name (and nicknames) can still be used by close family and friends.

JOKE

Who was the funniest pope?

Pope Hilarius

Latin for "cheerful," Pope Hilarius was elected in 461.

FUN FACT

Even though Peter was the birth name of eleven popes in Church history, there has never been a Pope Peter II.

Naming Groundbreaker

The pope can do anything he wants with his name, but most stick with tradition. Many choose to become the second, third (or even sixteenth!) pope to hold a given name. There have been a few papal name groundbreakers throughout the centuries.

Pope John Paul I was a papal name innovator. He was the first pope to choose a double name and the first who expected to be called "the first" during his lifetime. He always insisted on being called Pope John Paul I, when usually "the first" is only used after another pope takes the title. Do you think he knew something we didn't?

The first documented pope to change his name was Mercuricus. Named after the Roman god Mercury, he changed his name to John II because he didn't want to honor a pagan god. He was elected in 533.

Marcellus II was the last pope to have used his existing name (Marcello).

Does a Name Send a Message?

Sometimes, the popes choose their names because they want to send a message to the Catholic people and the world. The choice of a name can indicate what saint the pope wants to emulate, what types of policies he might enact during his reign, or even what his pastoral style might be.

Pope John Paul II chose his name to honor his predecessor, John Paul I, and in doing so indicated that he would continue his policies.

Pope Francis chose his name as a signal of his love for the poor and his desire to stand with them.

Pope Leo XIV chose his name to honor Pope Leo XIII, who wrote in support of the rights of workers during the Industrial Revolution, and because he recognizes that modern society poses "new challenges for the defense of human dignity, justice, and labor."

Top Papal Names

Papal Names QUICK FACTS

82
number of names used

139
popes keeping their previous names

46
names occurring only once

SIXTUS
first name to be used a second time

Papal Honorifics

If you find yourself in front of the pope someday, you'll want to know how to address him properly. The pope's full title is His Holiness _______ , Bishop of Rome, Vicar of Jesus Christ, Successor of the Prince of the Apostles, Supreme Pontiff of the Universal Church, Primate of Italy, Archbishop and Metropolitan of the Roman Province, Sovereign of the Vatican City State, Servant of the servants of God.

Since that's quite the mouthful, there are two other traditional options available. You can respectfully refer to the pope as either:

"Your holiness, Pope ____"

"Holy Father"

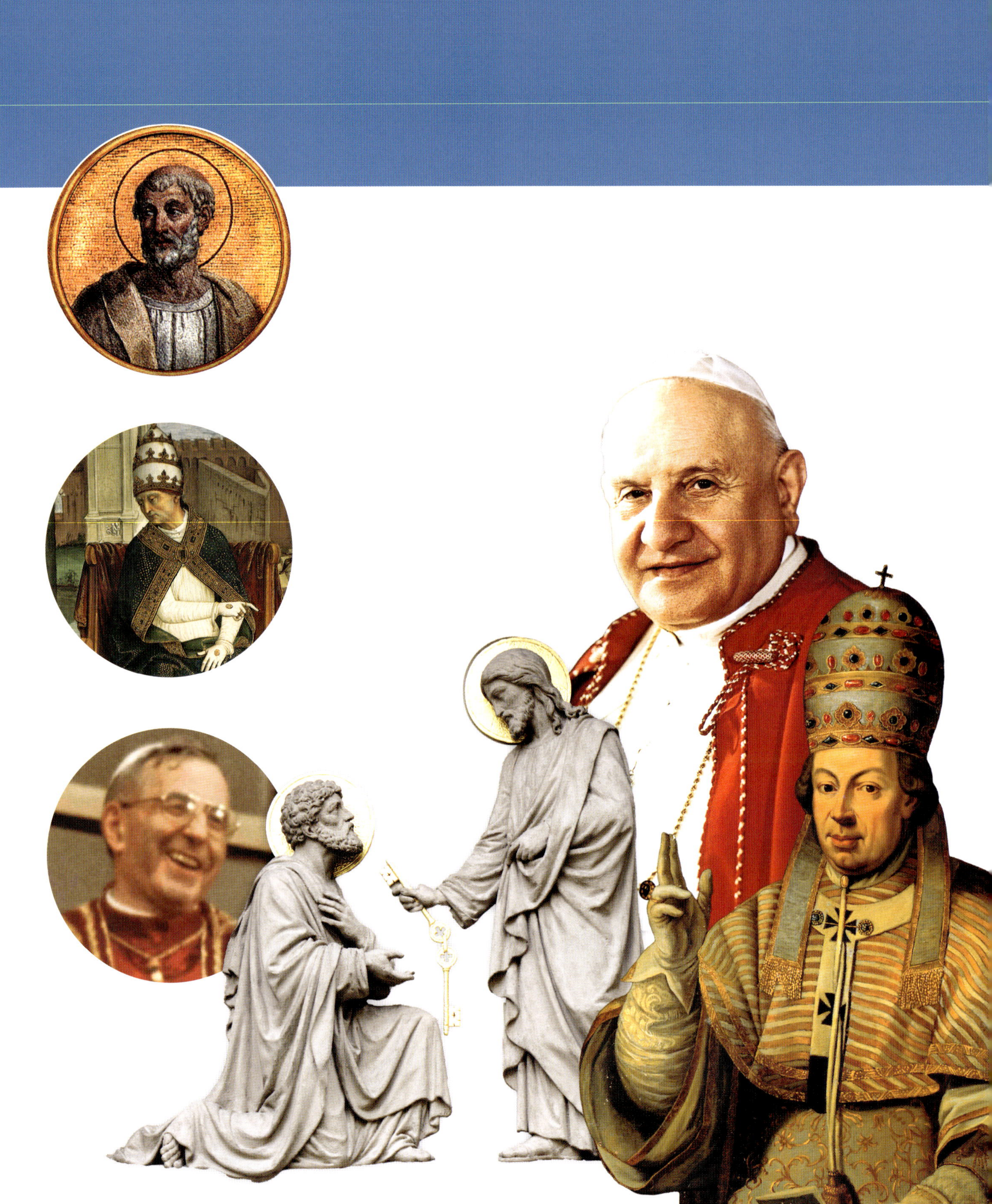

A Timeline of Popes

A Timeline of Popes

Popes in Chronological Order

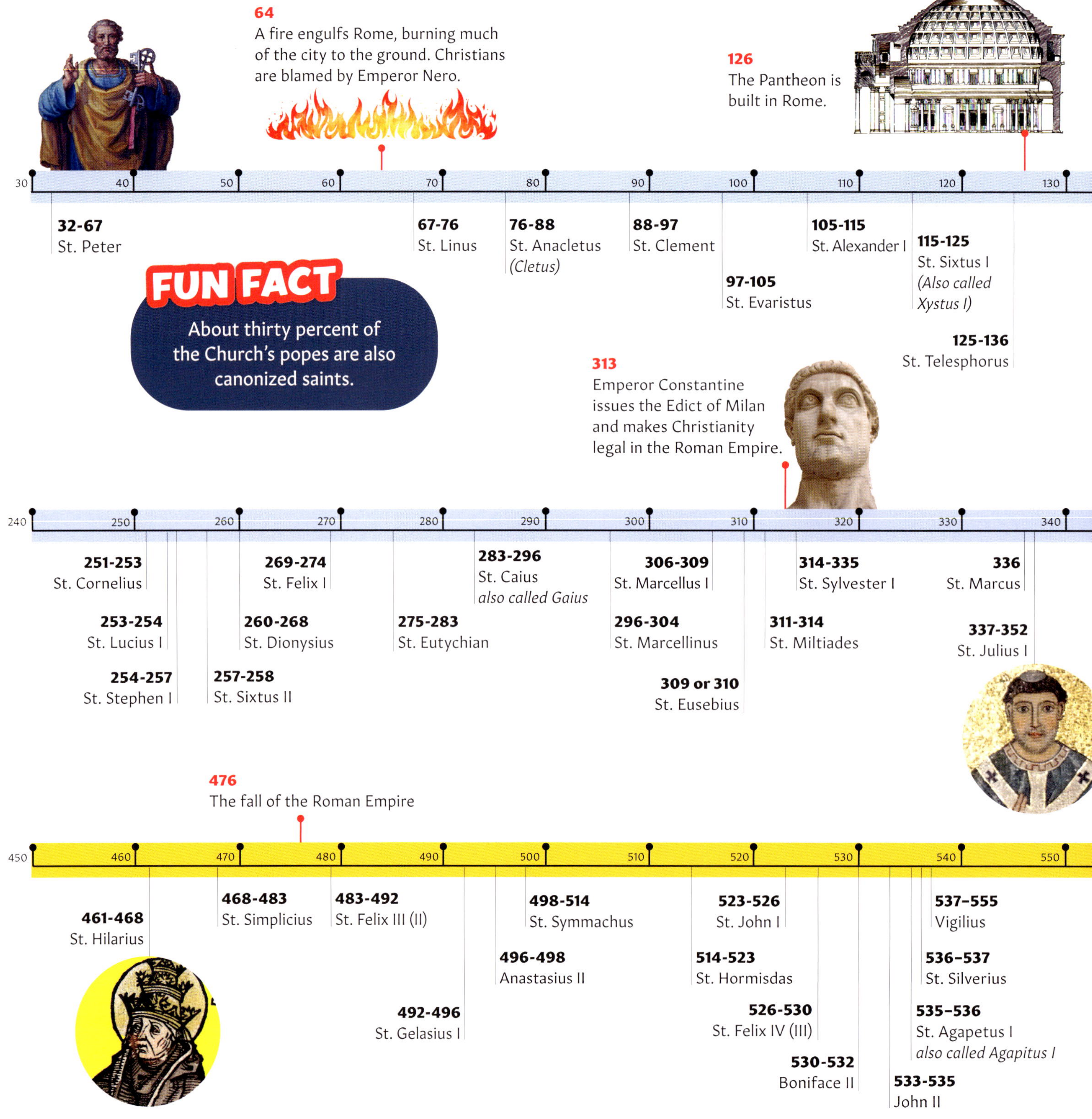

Color Key

- Early Popes
- Popes of the Middle Ages
- Popes of the Renaissance
- Early Modern Popes
- Modern Popes

220 China's Imperial Age begins.

140 150 160 170 180 190 200 210 220 230

136-140 St. Hyginus

140-155 St. Pius I

155-166 St. Anicetus

166-175 St. Soter

175-189 St. Eleutherius

189-199 St. Victor I

199-217 St. Zephyrinus

217-222 St. Callistus I

222-230 St. Urban I

230-235 St. Pontian

235-236 St. Anterus

236-250 St. Fabian

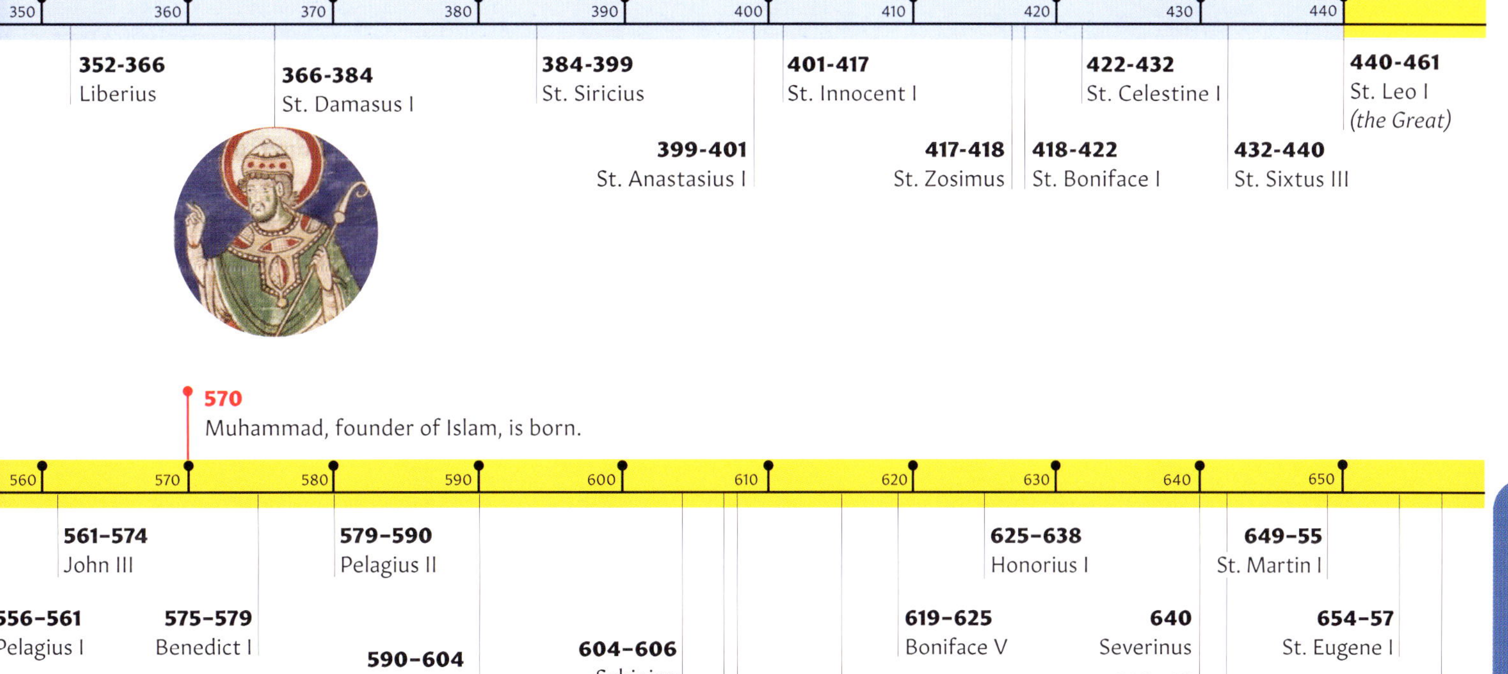

350 360 370 380 390 400 410 420 430 440

352-366 Liberius

366-384 St. Damasus I

384-399 St. Siricius

399-401 St. Anastasius I

401-417 St. Innocent I

417-418 St. Zosimus

418-422 St. Boniface I

422-432 St. Celestine I

432-440 St. Sixtus III

440-461 St. Leo I *(the Great)*

570 Muhammad, founder of Islam, is born.

560 570 580 590 600 610 620 630 640 650

556-561 Pelagius I

561-574 John III

575-579 Benedict I

579-590 Pelagius II

590-604 St. Gregory I *(the Great)*

604-606 Sabinian

607 Boniface III

608-615 St. Boniface IV

615-618 St. Deusdedit *(Adeodatus I)*

619-625 Boniface V

625-638 Honorius I

640 Severinus

640-42 John IV

642-49 Theodore I

649-55 St. Martin I

654-57 St. Eugene I

657-72 St. Vitalian

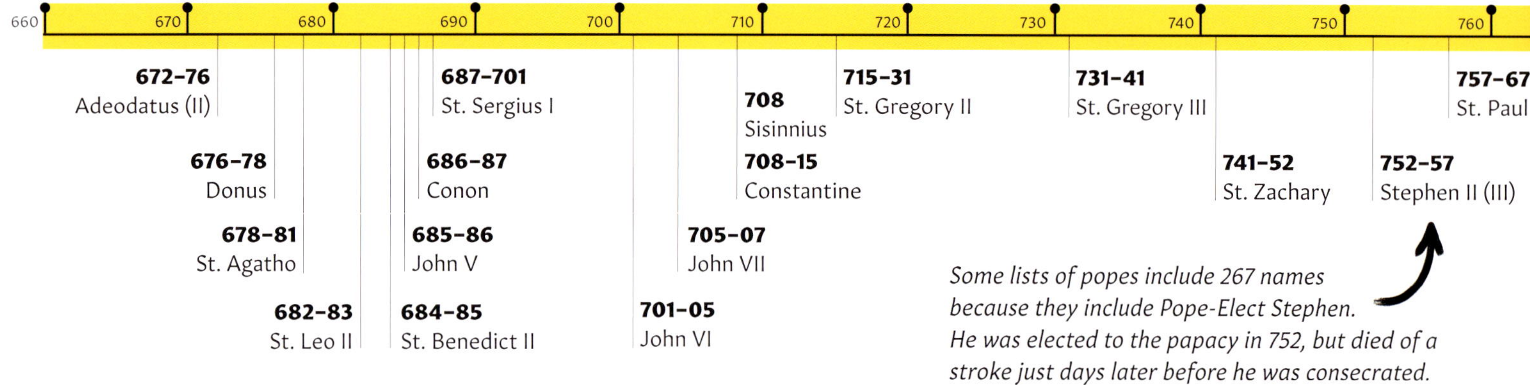
660
670
680
690
700
710
720
730
740
750
760
672–76
Adeodatus (II)
676–78
Donus
678–81
St. Agatho
682–83
St. Leo II
684–85
St. Benedict II
685–86
John V
686–87
Conon
687–701
St. Sergius I
701–05
John VI
705–07
John VII
708
Sisinnius
708–15
Constantine
715–31
St. Gregory II
731–41
St. Gregory III
741–52
St. Zachary
752–57
Stephen II (III)
757–67
St. Paul
Some lists of popes include 267 names because they include Pope-Elect Stephen. He was elected to the papacy in 752, but died of a stroke just days later before he was consecrated.

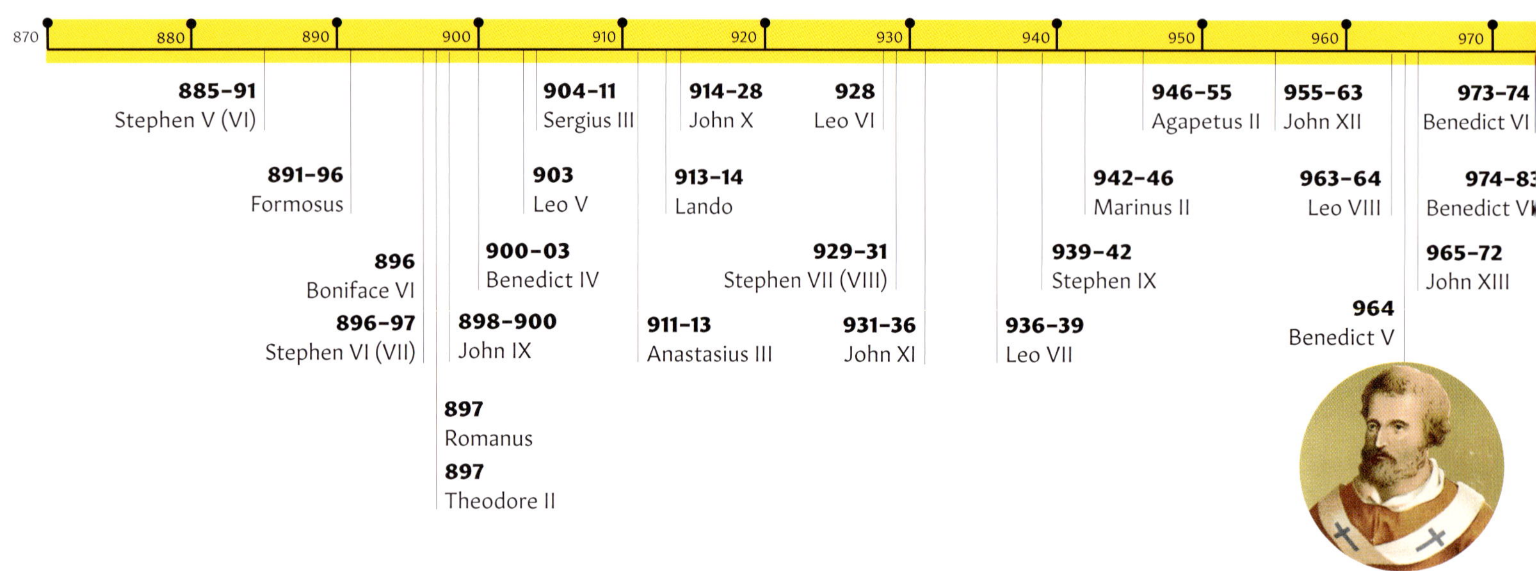
870
880
890
900
910
920
930
940
950
960
970
885–91
Stephen V (VI)
891–96
Formosus
896
Boniface VI
896–97
Stephen VI (VII)
897
Romanus
897
Theodore II
898–900
John IX
900–03
Benedict IV
903
Leo V
904–11
Sergius III
911–13
Anastasius III
913–14
Lando
914–28
John X
928
Leo VI
929–31
Stephen VII (VIII)
931–36
John XI
936–39
Leo VII
939–42
Stephen IX
942–46
Marinus II
946–55
Agapetus II
955–63
John XII
963–64
Leo VIII
964
Benedict V
965–72
John XIII
973–74
Benedict VI
974–83
Benedict VI

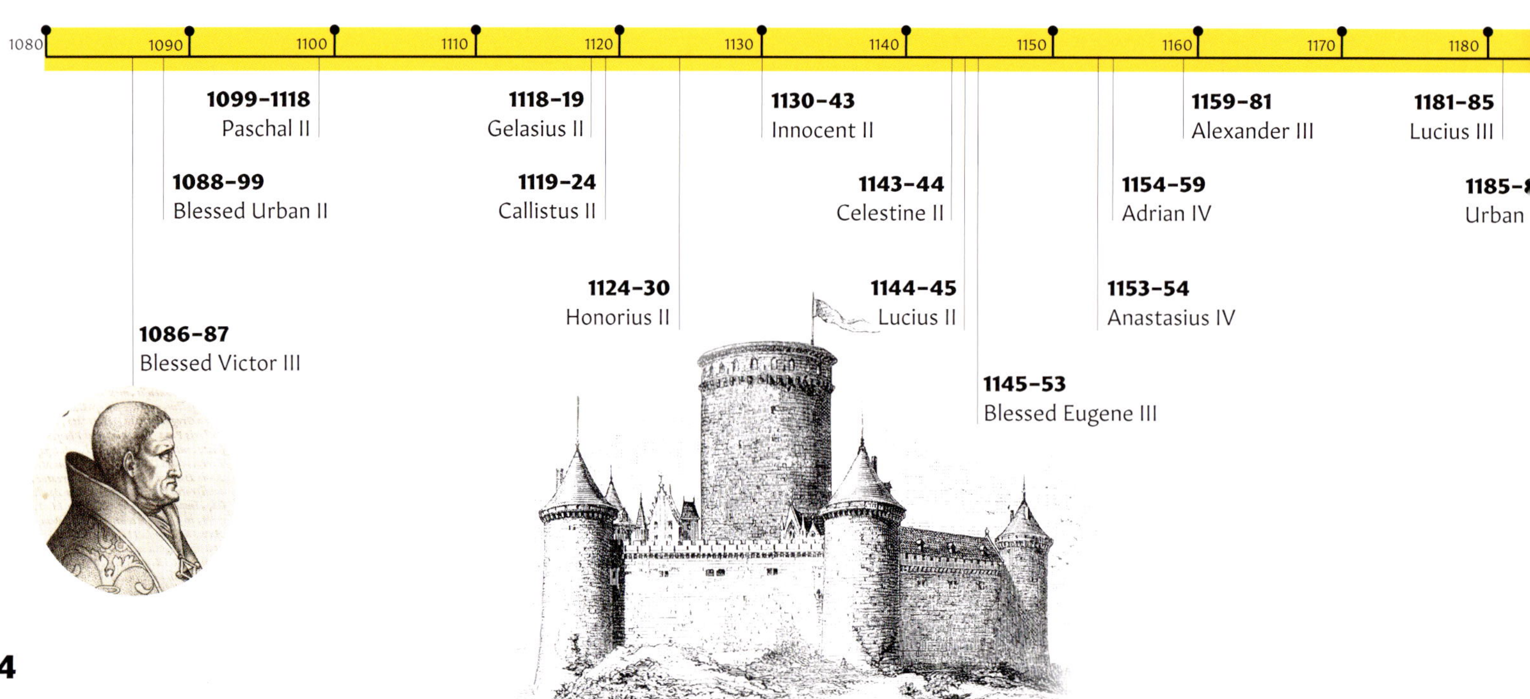
1080
1090
1100
1110
1120
1130
1140
1150
1160
1170
1180
1086–87
Blessed Victor III
1088–99
Blessed Urban II
1099–1118
Paschal II
1118–19
Gelasius II
1119–24
Callistus II
1124–30
Honorius II
1130–43
Innocent II
1143–44
Celestine II
1144–45
Lucius II
1145–53
Blessed Eugene III
1153–54
Anastasius IV
1154–59
Adrian IV
1159–81
Alexander III
1181–85
Lucius III
1185–
Urban

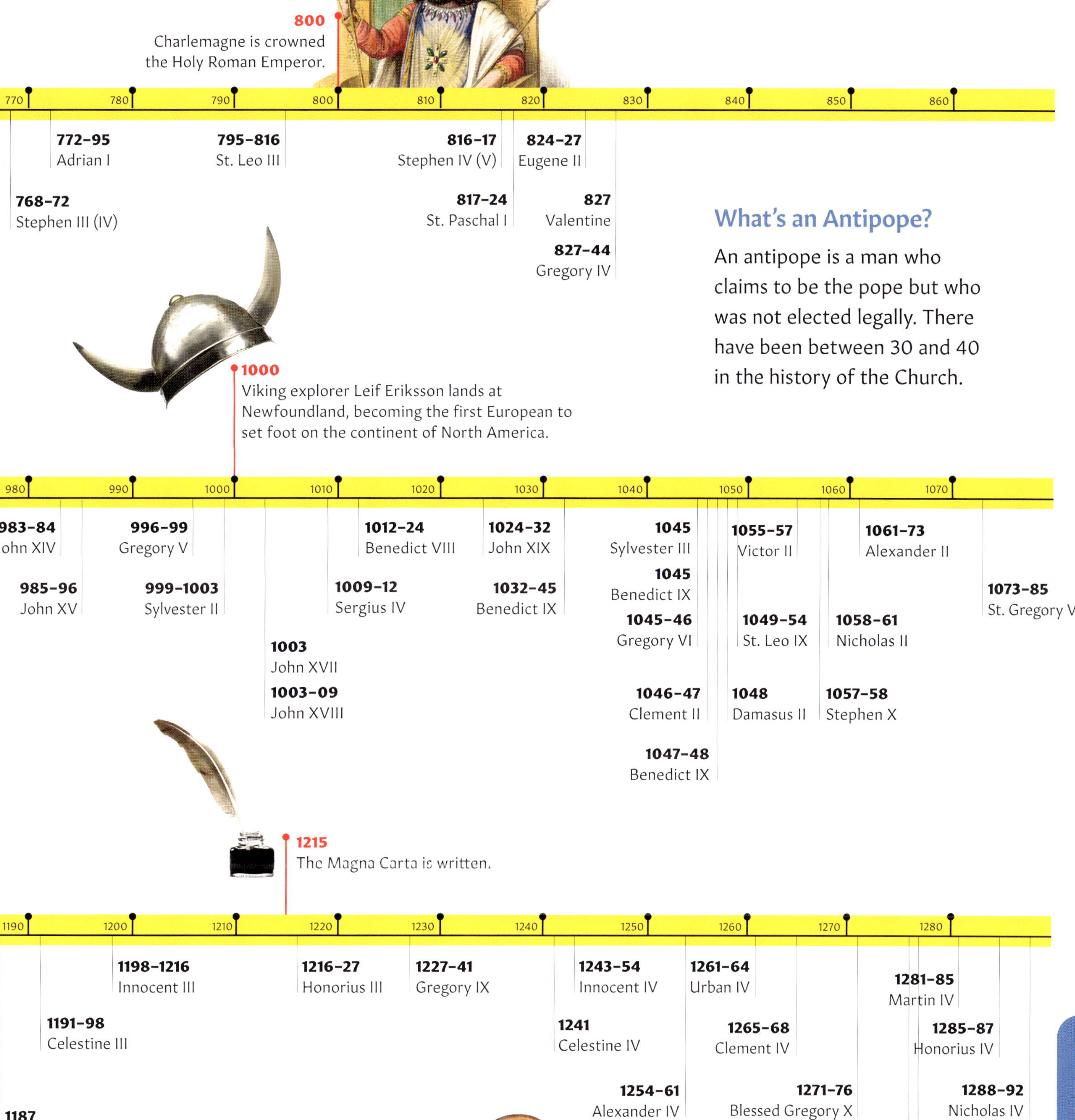

What's an Antipope?

An antipope is a man who claims to be the pope but who was not elected legally. There have been between 30 and 40 in the history of the Church.

Pope Nicholas III's corruption was so well known that he appears in Dante's Inferno, *doomed to hell for simony — the crime of buying and selling Church offices.*

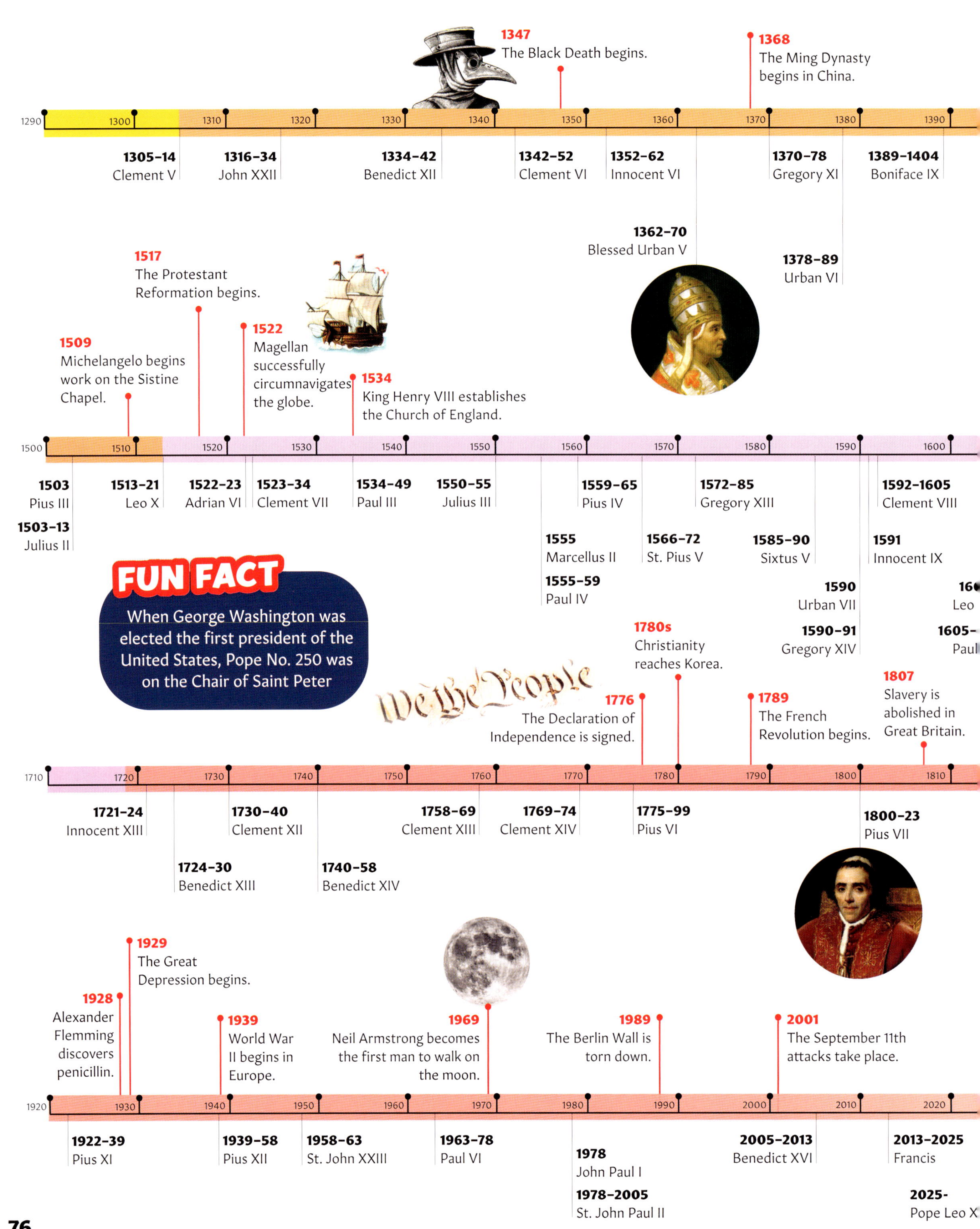

1347
The Black Death begins.
1368
The Ming Dynasty begins in China.
1290
1300
1310
1320
1330
1340
1350
1360
1370
1380
1390
1305–14
Clement V
1316–34
John XXII
1334–42
Benedict XII
1342–52
Clement VI
1352–62
Innocent VI
1370–78
Gregory XI
1389–1404
Boniface IX
1362–70
Blessed Urban V
1378–89
Urban VI
1517
The Protestant Reformation begins.
1509
Michelangelo begins work on the Sistine Chapel.
1522
Magellan successfully circumnavigates the globe.
1534
King Henry VIII establishes the Church of England.
1500
1510
1520
1530
1540
1550
1560
1570
1580
1590
1600
1503
Pius III
1503–13
Julius II
1513–21
Leo X
1522–23
Adrian VI
1523–34
Clement VII
1534–49
Paul III
1550–55
Julius III
1555
Marcellus II
1555–59
Paul IV
1559–65
Pius IV
1566–72
St. Pius V
1572–85
Gregory XIII
1585–90
Sixtus V
1590
Urban VII
1590–91
Gregory XIV
1591
Innocent IX
1592–1605
Clement VIII
Leo
1605–
Paul
FUN FACT
When George Washington was elected the first president of the United States, Pope No. 250 was on the Chair of Saint Peter
We the People
1776
The Declaration of Independence is signed.
1780s
Christianity reaches Korea.
1789
The French Revolution begins.
1807
Slavery is abolished in Great Britain.
1710
1720
1730
1740
1750
1760
1770
1780
1790
1800
1810
1721–24
Innocent XIII
1724–30
Benedict XIII
1730–40
Clement XII
1740–58
Benedict XIV
1758–69
Clement XIII
1769–74
Clement XIV
1775–99
Pius VI
1800–23
Pius VII
1929
The Great Depression begins.
1928
Alexander Flemming discovers penicillin.
1939
World War II begins in Europe.
1969
Neil Armstrong becomes the first man to walk on the moon.
1989
The Berlin Wall is torn down.
2001
The September 11th attacks take place.
1920
1930
1940
1950
1960
1970
1980
1990
2000
2010
2020
1922–39
Pius XI
1939–58
Pius XII
1958–63
St. John XXIII
1963–78
Paul VI
1978
John Paul I
1978–2005
St. John Paul II
2005–2013
Benedict XVI
2013–2025
Francis
2025-
Pope Leo X

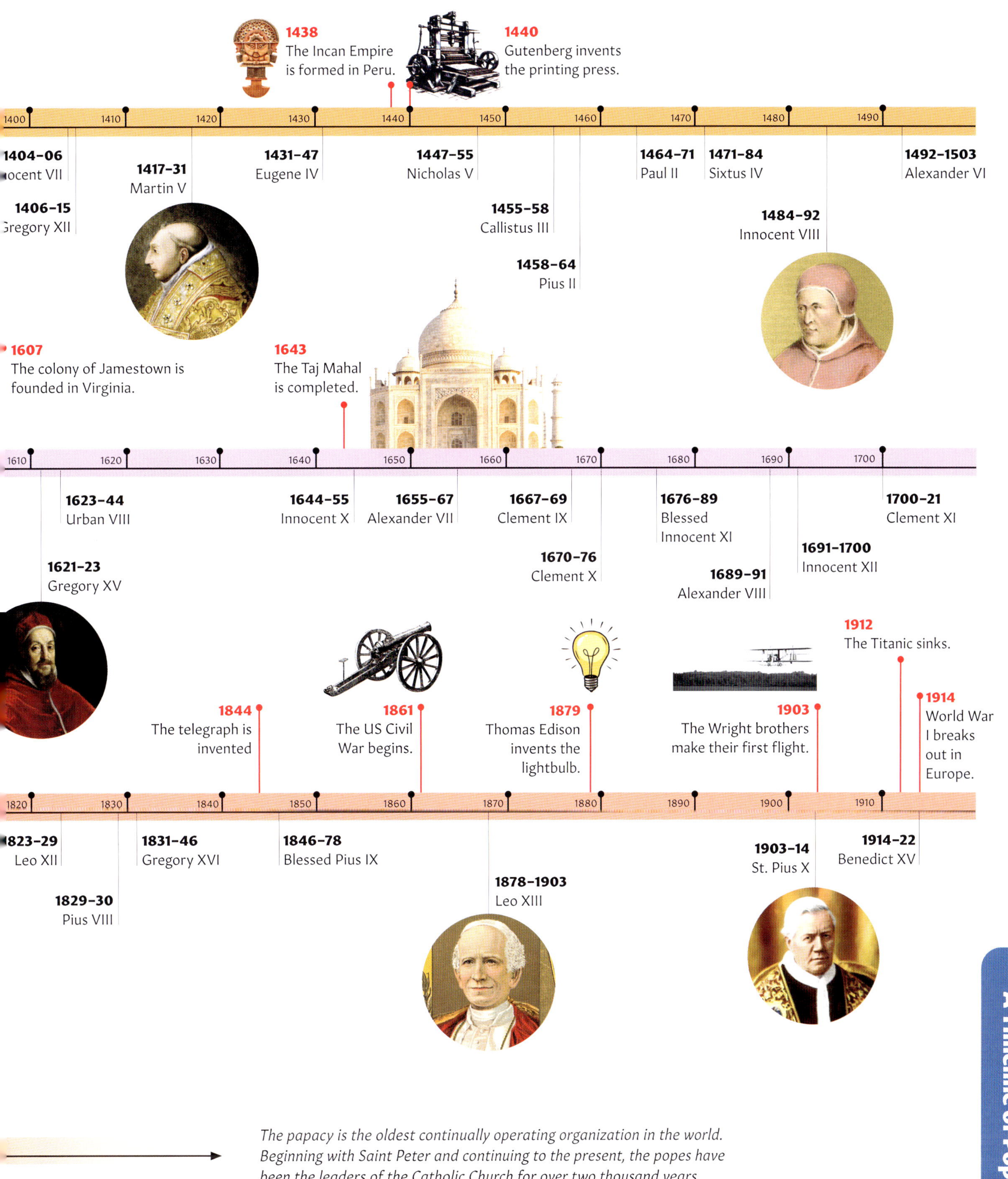

The papacy is the oldest continually operating organization in the world. Beginning with Saint Peter and continuing to the present, the popes have been the leaders of the Catholic Church for over two thousand years.

Early Popes

Because Christianity was illegal in the first centuries after Christ, many of the early popes were also martyrs. Very little is known about them or their reigns, apart from their names, though most are canonized saints.

Saint Peter

Papal Reign: 32–67

The very first pope, Saint Peter was chosen directly by Jesus and given the keys to the kingdom of heaven.

Pope Linus

Papal Reign: 67–76

Pope Linus was the first successor of Saint Peter after Saint Peter's death. He is mentioned in the Second Letter to Timothy as being a companion of Saint Paul. Tradition says he was buried next to Saint Peter.

FUN FACT

52 of the first 54 popes are canonized saints. The first non-saint pope? Pope Liberius (papacy 352-366).

Saint Peter's Tomb

Pope Pius XII authorized a series of archaeological excavations in the Vatican necropolis. The most astounding find of all was the tomb and remains of Saint Peter.

necropolis a large, elaborate cemetery of an ancient city

Pope Clement I

Papal Reign: 88–97

Pope Clement was the fourth pope of the Church. It is said that he was consecrated as a priest by Saint Peter. He wrote letters that still survive today that provide insight into the practices of the early Church.

Pope Anacletus

Papal Reign: 76–88

Also known as Cletus, Pope Anacletus is credited with creating twenty-five parishes in Rome.

Pope Miltiades

Papal Reign: 311–314

Both an African and a Roman citizen, Pope Miltiades was pope when Emperor Constantine made Christianity legal within the Roman Empire. The emperor presented him with the Lateran Palace, which then became the pope's residence.

Historical Note

In 313, Emperor Constantine made Christianity legal with the Edict of Milan.

Popes of the Middle Ages

The Middle Ages, also known as the medieval period, lasted for about one thousand years. This was a time of tremendous growth for Christianity. The Church was closely linked to the governments of each country and had the support of most of the kings and queens of Europe.

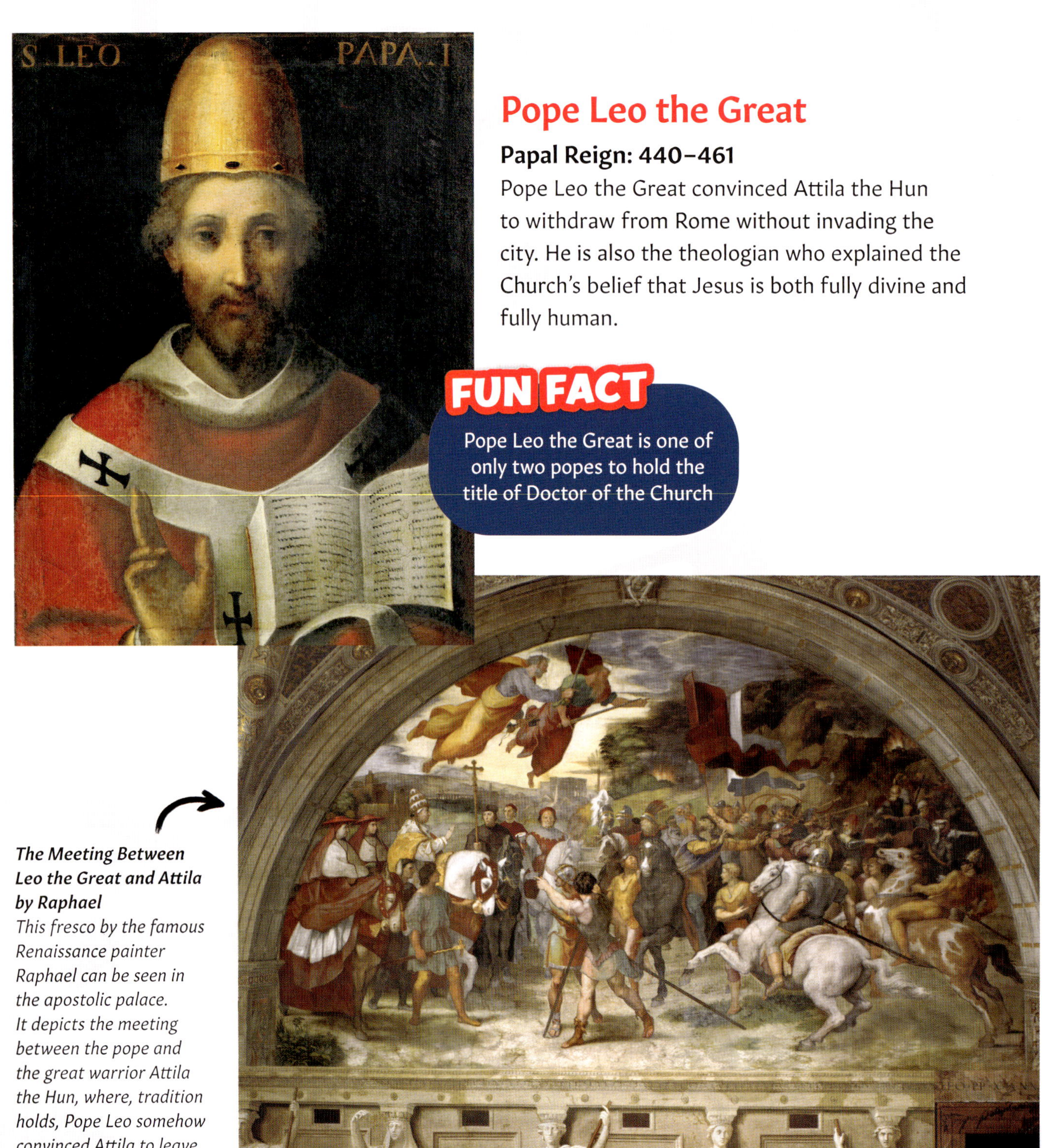

Pope Leo the Great

Papal Reign: 440–461

Pope Leo the Great convinced Attila the Hun to withdraw from Rome without invading the city. He is also the theologian who explained the Church's belief that Jesus is both fully divine and fully human.

FUN FACT

Pope Leo the Great is one of only two popes to hold the title of Doctor of the Church

The Meeting Between Leo the Great and Attila by Raphael

This fresco by the famous Renaissance painter Raphael can be seen in the apostolic palace. It depicts the meeting between the pope and the great warrior Attila the Hun, where, tradition holds, Pope Leo somehow convinced Attila to leave the city unharmed.

Pope Gregory I

Papal Reign: 590–604

Pope Gregory I, also known as Saint Gregory the Great, is the first pope that we know a lot about. This is because he wrote voluminously and many of his writings survive today.

Historical Note: The Papal States were created in 756, making the pope a powerful secular leader as well as the head of the Catholic Church.

Pope Leo III

Papal Reign: 795–816

Pope Leo III made waves in medieval Europe by crowning Charlemagne. At the time, Charlemagne was the Frankish king, an important position, but in crowning him at Saint Peter's, Leo did two world-changing things: First, he solidified Charlemagne as the head of what would become the Holy Roman Empire. Second, he set the precedent that only the pope could crown the emperor, putting the papacy above all secular governments, even empires.

Pope Benedict IX

Papal Reign: 1032–1044, 1045, 1047–1048

One of the Church's most infamous popes, Benedict IX remains the only man in history to hold the title three separate times. He was forced to resign after each of his elections because of his sinful behavior.

Popes of the Renaissance

The Renaissance Era in Europe spanned the fourteenth to seventeenth centuries. It was a time of rebirth for culture, art, science, and politics. Notably for the Catholic Church, the Protestant Reformation occurred during this period as well.

The Avignon Papacy

The Avignon Papacy is the period from 1309 until 1376, during which the papal court lived in Avignon, France, instead of Rome. At the time, the city states of Italy were largely at war with one another and French King Philip IV invited Pope Clement V to move to Avignon. Seven popes in total lived in France until Pope Gregory XI reestablished Rome as the papal capital. This set off the Western Schism and a series of antipopes held court in Avignon, France, until 1417.

The Great Schism

The Great Schism, also known as the Western Schism, was a period in Catholic Church history where there were two (sometimes three) men who claimed to be pope. It lasted from 1378 until 1417.

St. Catherine of Siena was instrumental in ending the Avignon Papacy. She traveled there herself and successfully convinced Pope Gregory XI to return to Rome.

Pope Martin V

Papal Reign: 1417–1431

The election of Pope Martin V to the papacy in 1417 ended the Great Schism. He was a Church reformer who sought to recover control of the Papal States and restore many of the Roman churches to their former glory.

Pope Pius II

Papal Reign: 1458–1464

Pope Pius II was a famed writer. His book *Commentaries* is the only known autobiography written by a pope. Pope Pius's book was translated into English and is still available today.

Pope Pius III

Papal Reign: 1503

Pope Pius III had one of the shortest papal reigns in history, lasting just under a month. Interestingly, he was not ordained a priest until after his election to the papacy. He died of a septic ulcer in his leg, though at the time of his death there were allegations that he had been poisoned.

Pope Julius II

Papal Reign: 1503–1513

One of the most influential popes of the Renaissance period, Julius II was an important patron of the arts. He commissioned Michelangelo's paintings in the Sistine Chapel and the art in the papal apartments today known as the Raphael Rooms (see page 58).

Early Modern Popes

The Early Modern Period is defined by many historians as lasting from about 1500 until 1700. Popes during these years oversaw the Church during a time of great upheaval and change. Important events within the Church during these centuries included the Protestant Reformation and the Counter-Reformation that followed.

Pope Leo X

Papal Reign: 1513–1521

Leo X was Pope when Martin Luther, a Catholic priest himself, posted his 95 Theses and began the Protestant Reformation. Much of what Luther was arguing against was corruption and excesses within Church hierarchy. Leo in particular had driven the Church into debt with his extensive military campaigns, construction projects, and his personal luxurious lifestyle.

Pope Adrian VI

Papal Reign: 1521–1523

Upon his election to the papacy, Adrian VI was determined to fix the excesses and corruption detailed by Martin Luther. Unfortunately, his reign was a short one, lasting just under two years, and his successor did not continue his efforts.

FUN FACT

Pope Adrian VI was Dutch and the last non-Italian pope to be elected until Pope John Paul II, 455 years later.

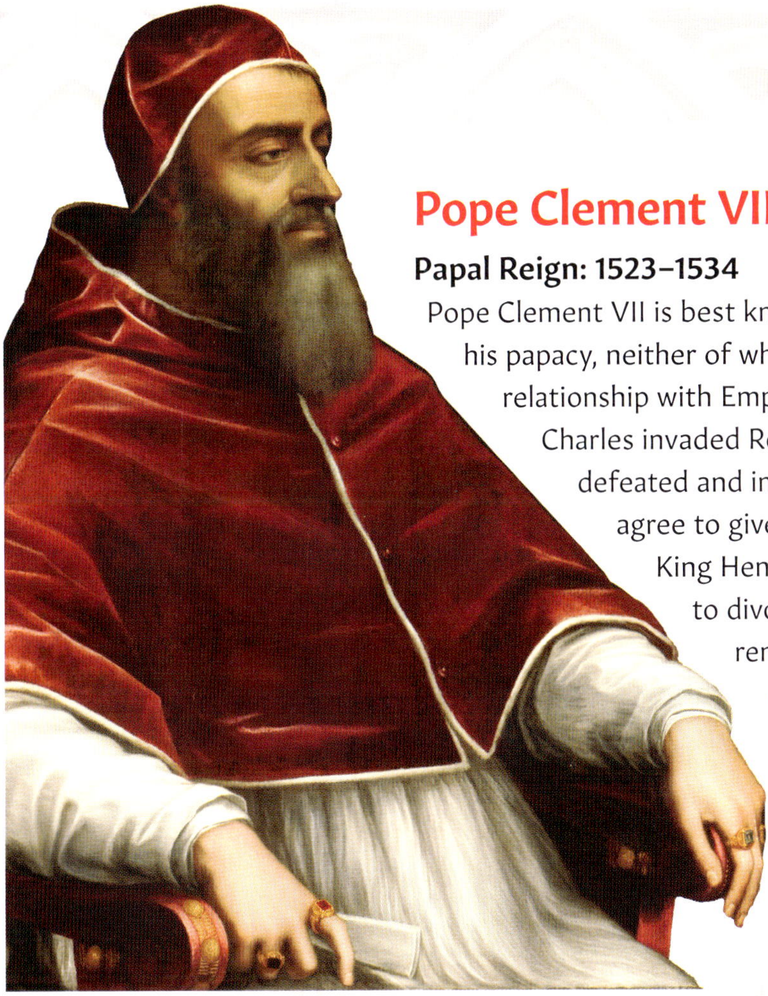

Pope Clement VII

Papal Reign: 1523–1534

Pope Clement VII is best known for two momentous events during his papacy, neither of which turned out as expected. By 1527, his relationship with Emperor Charles V had gotten so bad that Charles invaded Rome and laid siege to the Vatican. The defeated and imprisoned Clement had no choice but to agree to give up much of his power. At the same time, King Henry VIII of England, a Catholic, was hoping to divorce his wife, Catherine of Aragon, and remarry. In 1531, Pope Clement VII forbade the divorce under pain of excommunication. King Henry VIII went forward with his plan to divorce his wife and then issued a series of decrees that removed England from papal control and established the Anglican Church.

Pope Pius VI

Papal Reign: 1775–1799

Pope Pius VI was known as a reformer and careful administrator of the Papal States. He was elected to the papacy just a few months before the Declaration of Independence and would later erect the first diocese in the new United States of America in 1789 — the Diocese of Baltimore. When Napoleon conquered Italy, Pope Pius VI refused to concede power. He was taken captive and died a prisoner.

Modern Popes

Recent popes have been some of the most fascinating in history.

Pope Pius IX

Papal Reign: 1846–1878

Pope Pius IX convened the First Vatican Council in 1868. In 1870, the Italian army took control of the city of Rome, making Pope Pius IX a prisoner inside the Vatican and dissolving the Papal States. He would spend the rest of his papacy within the walls of the Vatican.

Pope Leo XIII

Papal Reign: 1878–1903

Pope Leo XIII was the first pope to have his voice recorded (praying the Hail Mary) and the first pope to be filmed. (He was filmed blessing the inventor of the camera, W. K. Dickson.) A reform-minded pope, he is also well known for his encyclical *Rerum Novarum*, which deals with the dignity of the working class. Pope Leo also composed the Saint Michael Prayer and mandated that it be said at the end of each Mass.

FUN FACT

When the future Saint Thérèse wanted to enter the Carmelite order early, her father took her to Rome, where, during a papal audience, she begged Pope Leo XIII's permission.

Pope John XXIII

Papal Reign: 1958–1963

John XXIII was elected as a papal placeholder. The cardinals felt that he was too old to have a long reign and wouldn't do very much to change the Church. They were wrong. As pope, John XXIII opened the Second Vatican Council, ushering in a new era of reform within the Church.

The coronation of Pope John XXIII lasted five hours.

Pope John Paul I

Papal Reign: 1978

Known as the Smiling Pope, John Paul I was the first pope to take on two names. He was a fascinating man who wrote fiction, including a series of letters to fictional characters and famous people, both dead and alive. His reign would only last thirty-three days. His sudden death threw the Vatican into turmoil, and though medical experts have declared that he died of natural causes, there were many conspiracies surrounding his death, claiming that he was assassinated.

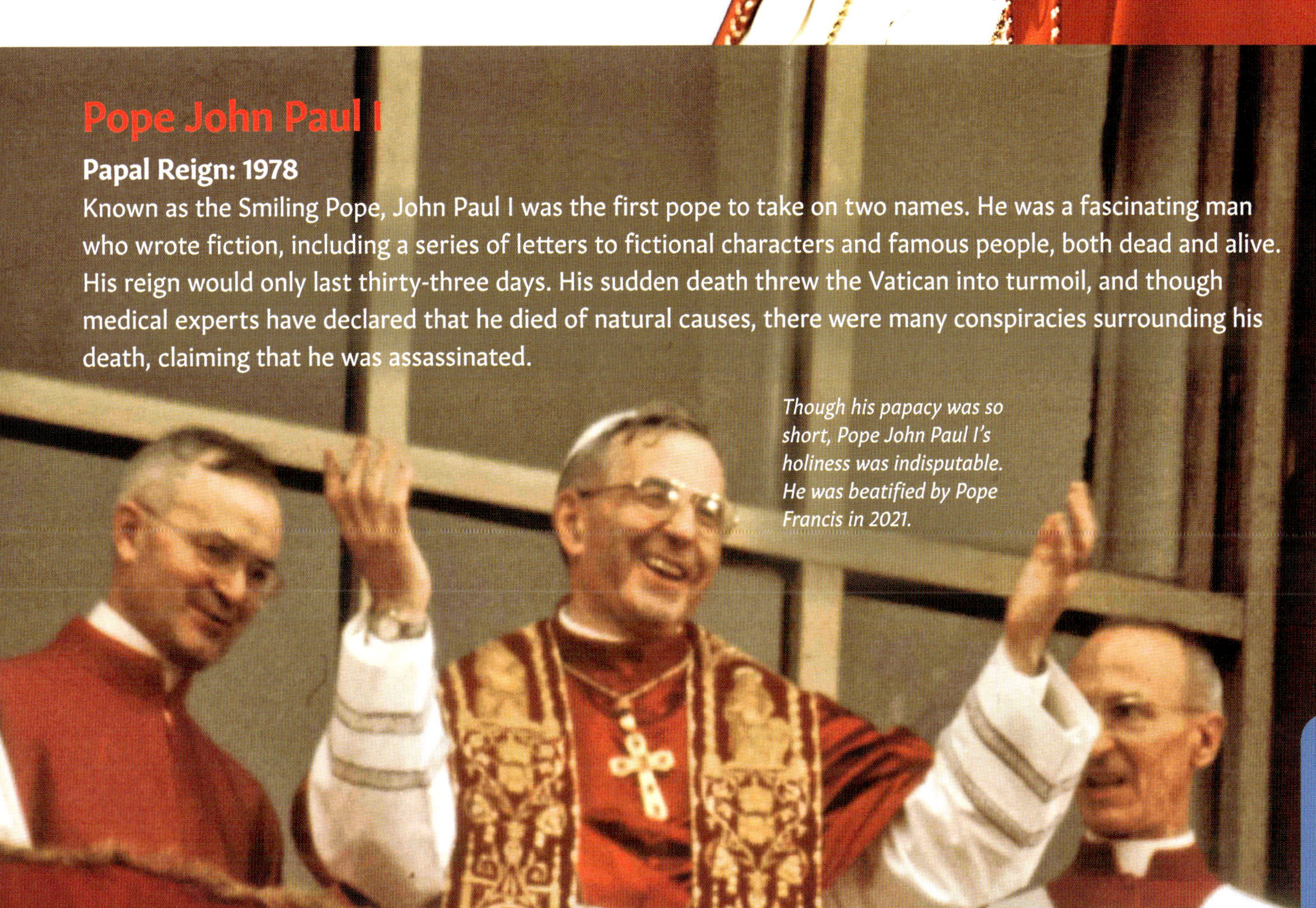

Though his papacy was so short, Pope John Paul I's holiness was indisputable. He was beatified by Pope Francis in 2021.

What's in a Name?

Choosing the name John was a controversial decision by Pope John XXIII. It had been over five hundred years since anyone had taken that name because the last man to do so had been antipope John XXIII. By taking the name, John XXIII confirmed the antipope status.

Pope John Paul II

Papal Reign: 1978–2005

Upon his election after the death of Pope John Paul I, Pope John Paul II became the first non-Italian pope in over four hundred years. A beloved man, Pope John Paul II was well known for his teaching on the theology of the body, his outreach to young people, and his devotion to Mary, the Mother of God.

As a young man, the future Pope John Paul II enjoyed the outdoors. He often hiked and skied with friends.

FUN FACT

The two popes who would follow John Paul II would also be from countries other than Italy.

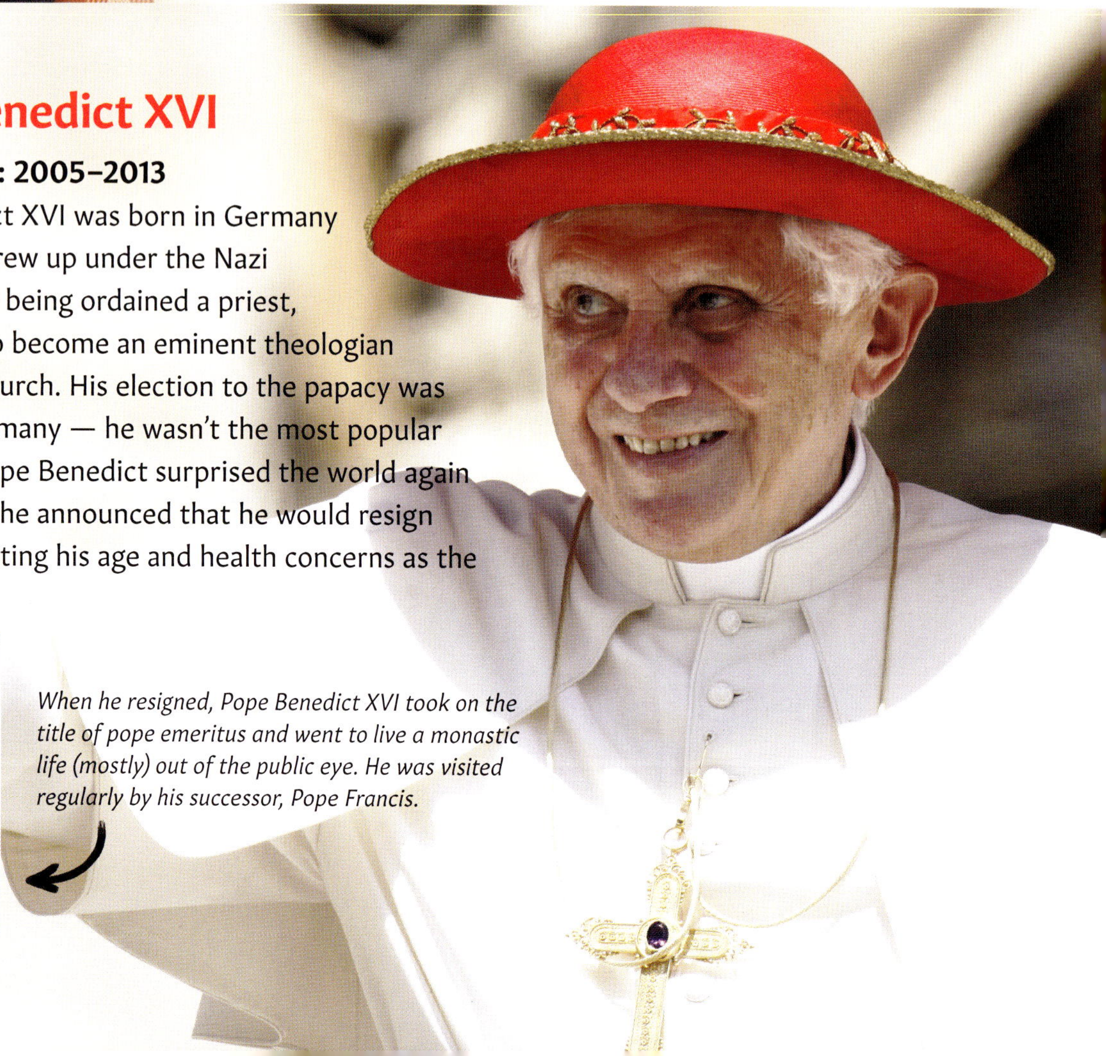

Pope Benedict XVI

Papal Reign: 2005–2013

Pope Benedict XVI was born in Germany in 1933 and grew up under the Nazi regime. After being ordained a priest, he went on to become an eminent theologian within the Church. His election to the papacy was a surprise to many — he wasn't the most popular candidate. Pope Benedict surprised the world again in 2013 when he announced that he would resign the papacy, citing his age and health concerns as the reasons.

When he resigned, Pope Benedict XVI took on the title of pope emeritus and went to live a monastic life (mostly) out of the public eye. He was visited regularly by his successor, Pope Francis.

Pope Francis

Papal Reign: 2013–2025

Pope Francis became the first pope from South America when he was elected in 2013. The first thing he did as pope, after blessing the crowds in Saint Peter's Square, was to ask the people gathered to pray for Pope Benedict XVI and for himself. He chose the name Francis to show solidarity with the poor. His papacy was marked by a focus on mercy and compassion.

One of the most iconic moments of his papacy was when Pope Francis delivered a special prayer and blessing in a completely empty Saint Peter's Square during the COVID pandemic.

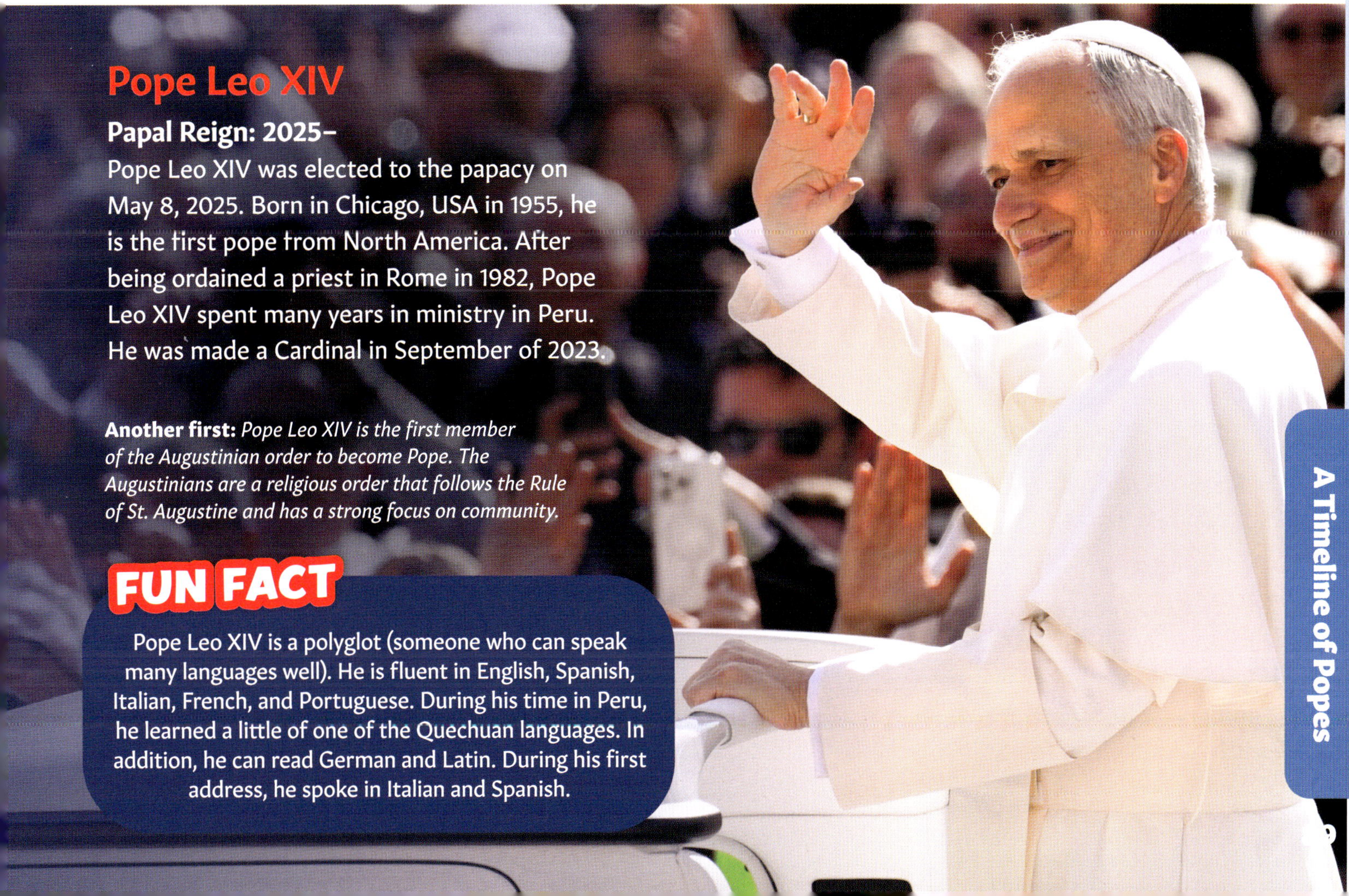

Pope Leo XIV

Papal Reign: 2025–

Pope Leo XIV was elected to the papacy on May 8, 2025. Born in Chicago, USA in 1955, he is the first pope from North America. After being ordained a priest in Rome in 1982, Pope Leo XIV spent many years in ministry in Peru. He was made a Cardinal in September of 2023.

Another first: *Pope Leo XIV is the first member of the Augustinian order to become Pope. The Augustinians are a religious order that follows the Rule of St. Augustine and has a strong focus on community.*

FUN FACT

Pope Leo XIV is a polyglot (someone who can speak many languages well). He is fluent in English, Spanish, Italian, French, and Portuguese. During his time in Peru, he learned a little of one of the Quechuan languages. In addition, he can read German and Latin. During his first address, he spoke in Italian and Spanish.

Index

R

S

T

U

V

Image Credits

PAGE 4: Adobe Stock **PAGE 5:** Dieter Philippi, Red Loafer of Pope Benedict XVI, Creative Commons share-alike 3.0 license; Alessia GIULIANI/CPP; Photo © NPL - DeA Picture Library / Bridgeman Images; Library of Congress **PAGE 6:** Adobe Stock; Photograph by Francesco Giordani **PAGE 7:** Adobe Stock **PAGE 8:** L to R – CNS photo/Paul Haring; CNS photo/Paul Haring; Photo © Photo Josse / Bridgeman Images; Photo © Stefano Baldini / Bridgeman Images; Adobe Stock **PAGE 9:** L to R – snipview.com; Adobe Stock; Photograph by Francesco Giordani **PAGE 10:** Top to Bottom – Pacific Press Media Production Corp. / Alamy Stock Photo; Paul Melling / Alamy Stock Photo **PAGE 11:** L to R – Peter Horree / Alamy Stock Photo; Archdiocese of Washington; Adobe Stock; Title page of the 1918 edition of the 1917 CIC, Wikimedia **PAGE 12:** Top to Bottom – Adobe Stock; The Calling of St. Peter, from a series of Scenes of the New Testament (fresco); Travellers & Tinkers, Creative Commons license 4.0 **PAGE 13:** Top to Bottom – Adobe Stock; Bridgeman Images **PAGE 14:** Top to Bottom – Photo © Raffaello Bencini / Bridgeman Images; Adobe Stock **PAGE 15:** Top to Bottom – Philadelphia Museum of Art: Saint Peter Released from Prison, 1370-1371, Jacopo di Cione; John G. Johnson Collection, 1917.; Crucifixion of Saint Peter by Caravaggio (c.1600), Wikimedia; Nero bust, Wikimedia **PAGE 16:** CLOCKWISE: Adobe Stock; OSV owned; Alessia Giuliani / CPP; Stefano Bianchetti / Bridgeman Images; Adobe Stock **PAGE 17:** Adobe Stock **PAGE 18:** Adobe Stock **PAGE 19:** Top to Bottom – Adobe Stock; Photo © The Holbarn Archive / Bridgeman Images **PAGE 20**: Top to Bottom – Christie's Images / Bridgeman Images; Tallandier / Bridgeman Images; Adobe Stock **PAGE 21:** L to R – Bridgeman Images; Farabola / Bridgeman Images; Lebrecht Music & Arts / Alamy Stock Photo; Adobe Stock **PAGE 22:** OSV owned; Adobe Stock; CNS photo/Lola Gomez © 2025, United States Conference of Catholic Bishops, All Rights Reserved **PAGE 23:** Adobe Stock; OSV owned, Adobe Stock **PAGE 24:** OSV owned; Adobe Stock **PAGE 25:** Adobe Stock **PAGE 26:** Adobe Stock; Adobe Stock; ©ALESSIA GIULIANI/CPP **PAGE 27:** Top to Bottom – Adobe Stock; Horizon Images/Motion / Alamy Stock Photo; ©MASSIMILIANO MIGLIORATO/Catholic Press Photo; Wikimedia **PAGE 28:** Chris Warde-Jones; Adobe Stock; UIG / Bridgeman Images **PAGE 29:** Photo by Lola Gomez, courtesy of Catholic News Service; Chris Warde-Jones; domonabikeItaly / Alamy Stock Photo; Alessia Giuliani / CPP **PAGE 30:** Adobe Stock; Stefano Bianchetti / Bridgeman Images; Anwar Hussein / Alamy Stock Photo **PAGE 31:** UPI / Alamy Stock Photo; Realy Easy Star / Alamy Stock Photo; Library of Congress; Adobe Stock **PAGE 32:** Top to Bottom – Library of Congress; CNS File; The Catholic news agency of the Bishops' Conference of Bosnia and Herzegovina; Public Domain/Wikimedia; Adobe Stock; The Portable Antiquities Scheme/ The Trustees of the British Museum, Creative Commons Share Alike 2.0 license; Adobe Stock **PAGE 33:** Adobe Stock **PAGE 34:** Top to Bottom – Stephen Barnes/ Religion / Alamy Stock Photo; The Catholic news agency of the Bishops' Conference of Bosnia and Herzegovina **PAGE 35:** Smith Archive / Alamy Stock Photo; The Portable Antiquities Scheme/ The Trustees of the British Museum, Creative Commons Share Alike 2.0 license; Property 12, Marin Luther excommunication; Adobe Stock **PAGE 36:** Top to Bottom – Adobe Stock; Christie's Images / Bridgeman Images **PAGE 37:** LaPresse / Alamy Stock Photo; Adobe Stock **PAGE 38:** Top to Bottom – Library of Congress; Farabola / Bridgeman Images; CNS File; Popular Graphic Arts Collection, Library of Congress; Forum / Bridgeman Images **PAGE 39:** Adobe Stock **PAGE 40:** Adobe Stock; KNA; Catholic Press Photo **PAGE 41:** Adobe Stock **PAGE 42:** Adobe Stock; OSV owned **PAGE 43**: Adobe Stock; Public Domain/Wikimedia **PAGE 44:** Catholic Press Photo; Adobe Stock **PAGE 45:** Adobe Stock **PAGE 46:** Top to bottom – MoiraM / Alamy Stock Photo; Agencja Fotograficzna Caro / Alamy Stock Photo; Wikimedia; DOD Photo / Alamy Stock Photo; Tim Graham / Alamy Stock Photo; Adobe Stock **PAGE 47:** Dieter Philippi, Red Loafer of Pope Benedict XVI, Creative Commons share-alike 3.0 license. **PAGE 48:** Top to bottom – ©VATICAN MEDIA /CPP; Giancarlo GIULIANI/CPP; Independent Photo Agency Srl / Alamy Stock Photo; ALESSIA GIULIANI/CPP **PAGE 49:** M. MIGLIORATO/CPP; M. MIGLIORATO/CPP; M. MIGLIORATO/ CPP; Adobe Stock **PAGE 50:** Agencja Fotograficzna Caro / Alamy Stock Photo; DOD Photo / Alamy Stock Photo; Tim Graham / Alamy Stock Photo; RealyEasyStar/ Fotografia Felici / Alamy Stock Photo **PAGE 51:** dpa picture alliance / Alamy Stock Photo; Photograph by Athanasius McVay; Photography courtesy of Papal Artifacts (papalartifacts.com); Dieter Philippi, Red Loafer of Pope Benedict XVI, Creative Commons share-alike 3.0 license. **PAGE 52:** Adobe Stock **PAGE 53:** CNS photo; CNS photo; CNS photo; CNS photo/Lola Gomez © 2025, United States Conference of Catholic Bishops, All Rights Reserved **PAGE 54:** Art Collection 2 / Alamy Stock; CPP; GIANCARLO GIULIANI/CPP **PAGE 55:** MoiraM / Alamy Stock Photo; Alessia GIULIANI/CPP; Wikimedia; photograph by Livioandronico 2013, Creative Commons 4.0 International license; Allstar Picture Library Ltd / Alamy Stock Photo **PAGE 56:** Design Pics Inc / Alamy Stock Photo; Adrian Wojcik / Alamy Stock Photo; Adobe Stock **PAGE 57:** Bailey-Cooper Photography / Alamy Stock Photo; adam eastland / Alamy Stock Photo **PAGE 58:** Album / Alamy Stock Photo; VM/CPP; VM/CPP **PAGE 59:** Adobe Stock; Adobe Stock; CPP **PAGE 60:** ALESSIA GIULIANI/CPP; Public domain. Source credit: From Nordisk Familjebok, vol. 8 (1908) on runeberg.org.; Abaca Press / Alamy Stock Photo; Adobe Stock; OSV owned **PAGE 61:** Alessia GIULIANI/CPP **PAGE 62:** ALESSIA GIULIANI/CPP; ALESSIA GIULIANI/CPP; Pope Leo's Ring –From *Nordisk Familjebok*, vol. 8 (1908) on runeberg.org. **PAGE 63:** ©Massimiliano MIGLIORATO / CatholicPressPhoto; VATICAN MEDIA/CPP **PAGE 64:** ABACAPRESS / Alamy Stock Photo; Adobe Stock **PAGE 65:** CNS photo/Nancy Phelan Wiechec; Alessia GIULIANI/CPP; AP Photo/Oded Balilty **PAGE 66:** ©ServizioFotograficoOR/CPP; CNS/Lola Gomez **PAGE 67:** Adobe Stock; OSV owned; Public Domain, Wikimedia **PAGE 68:** CNS photo; Portrait of Pope Marcellus II Cervini, Wikimedia Commons, public domain. has context menu; PVDE / Bridgeman Images; CNS file photo; CNS photo/Paul Haring; CNS/Lola Gomez **PAGE 70:** Top to Bottom – PVDE / Bridgeman Images; Universal Images Group North America LLC / DeAgostini / Alamy Stock Photo; Photo © NPL - DeA Picture Library / Bridgeman Images; Photo © Photo Josse / Bridgeman Images; Adobe Stock; © Marka/Universal Images Group / Bridgeman Images **PAGE 71:** Photo © NPL - DeA Picture Library / Bridgeman Images; Library of Congress **PAGE 72 & 73:** In chronological order – Adobe Stock; Adobe Stock; Adobe Stock; PVDE / Bridgeman Images; Adobe Stock; Adobe Stock; Oleografia Panigati e Meneghini Milano, CCO 1.0; Hugo DK, Creative Commons 4.0 license; Public Domain, Wikimedia; Public Domain, Wikimedia; Public Domain, Wikimedia **PAGE 74 & 75:** Adobe Stock; Municipal Library of Trento, Creative Commons CC0 1.0; Adobe Stock; Municipal Library of Trento, Creative Commons CC0 1.0; Adobe Stock; Adobe Stock; Saliko, Creative Commons 3.0 license. **PAGE 76 & 77:** Adobe Stock; Public Domain, Wikimedia; Galleria Colonna; Adobe Stock; Adobe Stock; Municipal Library of Trento, Creative Commons CC0 1.0; Adobe Stock; Public Domain, Wikimedia; Adobe Stock; Adobe Stock; Photo © Photo Josse / Bridgeman Images; Adobe Stock; Metropolitan Museum of Art, open access; Adobe Stock; Adobe Stock; Sconosciuta **PAGE 78:** Adobe Stock; PVDE / Bridgeman Images **PAGE 79:** PVDE / Bridgeman Images; PVDE / Bridgeman Images; PVDE / Bridgeman Images; Adobe Stock **PAGE 80:** © Veneranda Biblioteca Ambrosiana/Mondadori Portfolio / Bridgeman Images; © Vincenzo Pirozzi / Bridgeman Images **PAGE 81:** Adobe Stock; Photo © CCI / Bridgeman Images; Photo © NPL - DeA Picture Library / Bridgeman Images **PAGE 82:** Adobe Stock; Historic Images / Alamy Stock Photo **PAGE 83:** Fototeca Gilardi / Bridgeman Images; Photo © NPL - DeA Picture Library / Bridgeman Images; Photo © NPL - DeA Picture Library / Bridgeman Images; Michelangelo and Pope Julius II (oil on canvas) by Fontebuoni, Anastasio (c.1580-1626), Bridgeman Images **PAGE 84:** Portrait of Leo X, by Raphael. Wikimedia Commons, public domain; Pope Clement VII, painting by Sebastiano del Piombo; Portrait of Pope Adrian VI (after Jan van Scorel) Wikimedia **PAGE 85:** Pope Clement VII, painting by Sebastiano del Piombo; © Photo Josse / Bridgeman Images **PAGE 86:** Top to Bottom – CNS file photo; Library of Congress **PAGE 87:** DEA PICTURE LIBRARY / Alamy Stock Photo; © Marka/Universal Images Group / Bridgeman Images **PAGE 88:** Top to Bottom – CSI Productions / Alamy Stock Photo; ALESSIA GIULIANI/CPP; VaticanMedia-Foto/CPP **PAGE 89:** ©MASSIMILIANO MIGLIORATO/CPP; Abaca Press / Alamy Stock Photo; CNS photo/Lola Gomez © 2025, United States Conference of Catholic Bishops, All Rights Reserved

About the Author

Colleen Pressprich is a former missionary and Montessori teacher turned homeschooling mom and aunt. She is the author of several books for children and families including *Marian Consecration for Families with Young Children, The Jesse Tree for Families*, and *OSV Kids Stations of the Cross*. She and her husband live in Michigan where they raise their five kids and get to enjoy the sun approximately once every winter. You can find more about her on her website, elevatortoheaven.com.